David Young Bagby

Jesus the Nazarene is Certainly the Messiah of Jewish Prophecy

David Young Bagby

Jesus the Nazarene is Certainly the Messiah of Jewish Prophecy

ISBN/EAN: 9783337038502

Printed in Europe, USA, Canada, Australia, Japan

Cover: Foto ©Lupo / pixelio.de

More available books at **www.hansebooks.com**

JESUS THE NAZARENE

—IS—

CERTAINLY THE MESSIAH

—OF—

JEWISH PROPHECY.

BY REV. D. Y. BAGBY, PH.D.,

Author of "A Short History of the New Testament: or How the New Testament Writings Have Been Kept Since the Apostles," "Rome in Prophecy," "Bible Baptism," etc., etc.

LOUISVILLE, KY.:
BAPTIST BOOK CONCERN,
1897.

MANY OTHER SIGNS THEREFORE DID JESUS IN THE PRESENCE OF THE DISCIPLES, WHICH ARE NOT WRITTEN IN THIS BOOK: BUT THESE ARE WRITTEN, THAT YE MAY BELIEVE THAT JESUS IS THE CHRIST, THE SON OF GOD; AND THAT BELIEVING YE MAY HAVE LIFE IN HIS NAME.—JOHN 20:30,31.

INTRODUCTION.

"HAVING good, give." The author has found the real Good, and in these pages, proffers to give. "Oh! that I knew where I might find Him," has been the unuttered cry of the weary millions. To that way-worn and foot-sore throng this little volume offers to be the guide to His dwelling place. Many have found Him and are singing:

> "Jesus the very thought of thee,
>   With sweetness fills my breast;
> But sweeter far thy face to see,
>   And in thy presence rest."

To find Him, to know Him, is more than all besides. In this world's solitariness, ruin, sin, we need Him in his saving grace, in His preserving care, in His guiding eye, in His shaping hand, in His changeless love, and in His gathering arms.

What a boon then is Christ to any smitten, seared, and scarred soul!

> "When I found Him in my bosom,
>   Then I found Him everywhere;
> In the bud and in the blossom,
>   In the earth and in the air."

Oh! that many may read, and that every reader may thereby find Him!

A. C. DAVIDSON.

GEORGETOWN COLLEGE, KY.,
    May 25, 1897.

TABLE OF CONTENTS.

THE SUBJECT STATED.

1. Testimony of the Old Testament in General, ... 10
2. The Object of this Book, ... 11
3. God *Only* Can Foretell the Future, ... 13

PART I.
THE PROPHECIES EXAMINED.

CHAPTER I.
THE COMING MESSIAH.

1. General Promises of His Coming, ... 17
2. Time of His Appearance, ... 19
   (1.) To be Before Judah Ceased to Rule, ... 19
   (2.) Certain Years *After* the Temple Should be Rebuilt, ... 20
3. Place of His Birth, ... 22
   (1.) The Town Named, ... 22
   (2.) This Town so Understood as His Birthplace, ... 23
4. Manner of His Birth, ... 24
   (1.) Messiah's "Sign," 24
   (2.) Messiah's Names, ... 26

CHAPTER II.
MESSIAH'S RECEPTION IN THE WORLD.

1. The Magi to Worship, ... 29
2. Persecuted at Birth, ... 29
3. To be Driven from His Native Country, ... 30

CHAPTER III.
NATURES OF THE COMING MESSIAH.

1. His Human Nature: His Ancestry, ... 33
    (1.) His Earliest Ancestry Named, ... 33
        a. To be of Abraham's Seed, ... 34
        b. Of the Seed of Isaac, ... 34
        c. And of the Seed of Jacob, ... 35
        d. And the Seed of Judah, ... 35
    (2.) His Later Ancestry Named, ... 36
        a. To be of the Seed of Jesse, ... 37
        b. And of the Seed of David, the King, 37
2. His Divine Nature: His Divinity, ... 39

CHAPTER IV.
MESSIAH AND HIS DOCTRINES.

1. His Gentleness, ... 44
    (1.) As a Tender Shepherd, ... 45
    (2.) A Man of Meekness, ... 46
    (3.) Will be Pleasing to God, ... 48
2. Will be Patient Under All Trials, ... 49
    (1.) He Will be Sorely Maltreated, ... 50
    (2.) He Will be Silent When Afflicted, ... 52
    (3.) He Will Pray for His Enemies, ... 53
3. Messiah's Doctrines, ... 55
    (1.) His Sceptre One of Righteousness and Love, ... 55
    (2.) Regeneration Promised, ... 57
    (3.) The Holy Spirit to be Sent, ... 59

CHAPTER V.
MESSIAH'S LIFE AND LABORS.

1. Beginning of His Kingdom, ... 61
    (1.) The Forerunner, ... 61

(2.) The Wilderness Cry, ... 62
(3.) The Way Prepared, ... 63
2. Messiah to be a Preacher of the Gospel, ... 67
3. Messiah to be a Great Light, ... 71
4. Messiah to be a Healer of the Afflicted, ... 72
5. To Triumphantly Enter the Jewish Capital, ... 75
6. And He Will Be Rejected, ... 76

CHAPTER VI.
MESSIAH'S ARREST AND DEATH.

1. The Betrayal, ... 84
   (1.) The Betrayer, ... 85
   (2.) The Price Paid, ... 87
   (3.) Disposition of Price Paid, ... 88
   (4.) The "Shepherd Smitten: The Sheep Scattered," 89
2. The False Witnesses, ... 90
3. Treatment at the Cross, ... 91
   (1.) What Messiah Himself Will Do, ... 92
      a. Will Suffer for Others, ... 92
      b. He Will Intercede for His Persecutors, ... 94
      c. Messiah Will Cry Unto God, ... 95
      d. Will Die with Malefactors, ... 96
   (2.) What Others Will Do Unto Messiah, ... 98
      a. Will Pierce His Hands and His Feet, 98
      b. Will Give Him Vinegar to Drink, .. 99
      c. Will Divide His Garments: Cast Lots for His Coat, ... 100
      d. Will Break No Bone, But Pierce Him, ... 101
      e. Will Deride Him, ... 103
      f. And Bury Him with the Rich, ... 104

CHAPTER VII.
MESSIAH TO RISE FROM THE DEAD.

1. His Resurrection, ... 107
2. Messiah's Ascension, ... 110

CHAPTER VIII.
HIS KINGDOM TO SPREAD THE WORLD OVER.

1. To be a Missionary Kingdom, ... 113
2. Mission Work Done by His Converts, ... 117

CHAPTER IX.
SOME NEGATIVE VIEWS OF THE LIFE OF JESUS.

Some Things Which Could Not Have Been True of an Impostor, ... 120

CHAPTER X.
SOME UNAVOIDABLE CONCLUSIONS, ... 131

PART II.
THE PROPHECIES FULFILLED.

The Old Testament Prophecies and the New Testament Fulfillments arranged in parallel columns, ... 135-178

JESUS THE NAZARENE IS THE MESSIAH OF PROPHECY.

THE SUBJECT STATED.

IT would seem that a subject as important to the follower of Jesus as this subject is, would have been discussed till the whole matter had become as familiar as the story of His birth, or His death on the cross; but when we attempt to find books on the subject, we learn that they are very few; in fact, this writer has not been able to find any one book wholly written on this theme. Two or three have chapters referring to this subject; but the whole thing has been neglected by the book writers; and this is a sufficient reason why the present writer now assumes the task of presenting this important theme to the public in the shape of a book. Do you accept Jesus as your Savior? How do you know that He is the One who was to come into the world to redeem the world from sin? Do you reject Jesus? How do you know but that He is the very One who was to come into the world on no other mission than to redeem you and all others like you from your sins? We hope to learn something on this question of a Messiah, ere we have finished this book.

1. THE TESTIMONY OF THE OLD TESTAMENT IN GENERAL.

No one can read the Old Testament with any degree of care without learning the fact that the authors of these writings were continually on the lookout for a Great and Glorious Personage, who was to come into the world, at some time in the future, for the purpose of restoring the people, in some way, to the favor of an offended God. So clearly was this seen by the Old Testament writers, that they wrote often and over again, of the coming Deliverer; they have given us many plain prophecies of His coming, and the more these writings are studied the more clearly is the fact seen that all the Old Testament writers had this event in view as they penned their sacred words. In an obscure way, the fact of the coming of some Great Sin-bearer was announced to the first human pair (Gen. 3:15), and as the world grew older, the prophecies were multiplied, and not only did they become more numerous, but they also became more definite and pointed, with a growing accuracy towards a certain Person, and to a definite *time when* He should come to redeem the people from their sins.

These prophecies began to be written as far back as the days of Moses, fifteen hundred years before our Christian era, and some of them were announced to the world more than four hundred years before that date, and one (above cited) was made near *four thousand* years before the beginning of our present era; and continually from that date of Moses, with longer or shorter intervals intervening, the prophecies were multiplied concerning this Great Redeemer, up to within four hundred years of our era, at which time (400 B. C.) they ceased altogether.

2. THE OBJECT OF THIS BOOK.

It is the design of this book to examine and study these prophecies in as candid and unbiased a manner as it can be done, and learn, if possible, who fulfilled them, and when it was done; and, further, if they are not fulfilled yet, to see if there is a possibility of their being fulfilled.

We shall learn that there are a number of

surroundings in which the Redeemer *must* come, in order to fulfill these prophecies; for instance, some of them tell us plainly who will be in power, and who have passed out of power, as well as the condition of the Jewish worship at the time when the great Deliverer shall make His appearance in the world.

Now, it is certainly clear to any candid mind, that if these conditions have already come, have continued for a while, and have passed away, and passed so completely that it is practically impossible for them ever to return; as this can be shown easily; for when certain nations have come and died away they can not exist again, any one knows; that also the time for the coming Deliverer has come and passed as well; certainly if all the environment in which He had to come has already come and gone forever, and that it is impossible for these to be repeated, then we have the whole question reduced down to but two propositions, viz.:

1. There can never be a Redeemer; or
2. The Redeemer has already come.

With these two propositions stated so clearly that a child can comprehend them, let us proceed to investigate the prophecies themselves, and learn who has fulfilled them, and when it was done.

3. GOD ONLY CAN FORETELL THE FUTURE.

Let us bear in mind the fact, that in the very nature of the constituted world, that none but an Omniscient God *can* foretell the future. There may be, and in fact, there are some things which occur, that are ruled by the laws of Nature's own mathematics, which may be told before hand, such as the eclipses, the transits of certain planets, and such as are governed by the laws of unchanging nature. For instance, I may say now that in the year 2000, the sun will rise at six o'clock, March 21st; but the statement would not be a prophecy in the least; for this is ruled by the laws which have governed the motions of the earth ever since it was set in motion in its present orbit.

A prophecy is the foretelling of a future event, to which there is not, neither can there be, a mathematical clue for the solution of the problem, nor any other rule of natural law.

That a particular individual is to be born into the world, at a given time, and that he will perform certain specified deeds, and also that other things will be done to him; and all these foretold by men living from 400 to 2000 years before the event takes place, are facts that no man *can* know, unless he be guided by *Him* who governs all things after the counsel of His own will, even the Omniscient God of the Universe Himself. Who dares to dispute this statement?

In the future pages, we shall see what was said about the coming of the Great Personage: see what He will do, as well as learn what others will do unto Him; remembering, at the same time, that all these prophecies were predicted from 400 to 2000 years before they were fulfilled.

We shall take up the periods of the life of the coming Redeemer, and arrange them, with the prophecies, in their respective eras, that they may all stand out clearly and with their full force, collectively; then may we see them at a glance bearing on one point, and get all the power of their combined testimony.

Part I. examines the prophecies separately as well as connectedly, adding such comments as the writer may think necessary. Part II. collects all the prophecies that bear upon any one point or part of the life of the Messiah, arranging them together, and also placing the fulfillment in a parallel column, without any comment. Notes of explanation will be found at the bottom of pages in the first part, but not repeated in the second.

May the writer hope that there will be a careful and unprejudiced examination of these prophecies made by the reader, and that he or she will accept the testimony, and then act upon it in a way that will stand the test of both time and eternity?

If Jesus is the Messiah, the Christ, as they both mean the same thing, will it not be wise to accept Him, and follow Him all your days? And will it not be the height of folly to reject Him, and turn after the world and the pleasures thereof, when you run such a risk of being lost forever?

May God help us to read and study the book as for eternity; and if there is one soul brought to see Jesus as his or her Savior, or if any Christian is strengthened in his or her faith in the Lord Jesus by the book, the writer will be abundantly paid for the labor spent upon its preparation.

PART I.

THE PROPHECIES EXAMINED.

CHAPTER I.
THE COMING MESSIAH.

1. GENERAL PROMISES OF HIS COMING.

THERE are a number of promises that a Deliverer will come into the world at some time in the future, but with no definite data from which any idea can be obtained as to *when* this event shall occur. Such promises are given, not to enable any one to locate the time, but as an encouraging promise that He will surely come. Such passages as Num. 24:17, and some others similar, are of this kind: "I shall see Him, but not now: I shall behold Him, but not nigh: there shall come a Star out of Jacob, and a Sceptre shall rise out of Israel, and shall smite the corners of Moab." And again, the promise made to the first pair of human beings, when they had sinned, found in Gen. 3:15, as to the seed of the woman bruising the serpent's head; very indefinite, you may say, and so it is; but they understood it to refer to the Great Deliverer, as we may see from what Eve said when she had given birth to the first child ever born into the world, Gen. 4:1: "I have gotten a man, Jehovah." (Correct reading of Hebrew.)

Again, we find Isaiah saying, 59:20: "And a Redeemer shall come to Zion, and unto them that turn from transgression in Jacob, saith the Lord." Here again there is the promise that a Savior shall come, but no idea is given as to *when* He will appear upon the earth; but the promise stood as an encouragement to those of that day that there would come, some time, a Great Deliverer to help the people.

So we find that Hag. 2:7, said: "And I will shake all nations, and the Desire of all nations shall come: and I will fill this house with glory, saith the Lord."

While these prophecies are not so definite as to the time when Messiah was to come, yet taken with others, they are of value, and make the case stronger that there was certainly coming One who would redeem the people from their sins; and the people of those days knew that these passages referred to the Great and Mighty Deliverer of Israel.

2. TIME OF HIS APPEARANCE.

Besides these indefinite promises of His coming, we have some very clear and pointed prophecies as to *when* He might be expected upon the earth. The first definite one as to time, we find, is made more than two thousand years after the fall of Adam into sin, and it was made by Jacob.

(1.) TO BE BEFORE JUDAH CEASED TO RULE.

In the farewell which Jacob took of his sons, found recorded in Gen. 49:10, we find the first direct promise as to the time *when* Messiah should come. "The sceptre shall not depart from Judah, nor a lawgiver from between his feet, until Shiloh* come; and unto Him shall the gathering of the people be."

That is to say there shall be a ruler among the descendants of the children of Judah until the time when the Great Deliverer of Israel should come.

The special question to us is, Did Jesus appear in the world at the proper time to fulfill this

---

*The word here translated "Shiloh" is from the Hebrew (shalom) from "shalam," to be whole, safe, secure, and this form means "to be at peace" or "The peaceful One." It is the same word as is in Isa. 9:5: "Sar Shalom," "Prince of Peace," and is one of the names that was given to the Messiah by that prophet.

prophecy? Was He born into the world before the descendants of Judah ceased to rule? Of course, to decide this question, we must learn *when* He was born, and who was ruling at the time.

Josephus and the New Testament, as well as contemporary writers, tell us that Herod the Great was on the throne of Judah at the time when Jesus was born, and that his wife was Mariamne, the daughter of Alexandra, who was the daughter of Hyrcanus the high priest. This Herod died just after the birth of Jesus, as we learn from Matt. 2:19.

Jesus then fulfills completely this prophecy as to the time *when* the Messiah should be born into the world.

(2.) TO BE BORN CERTAIN YEARS AFTER THE TEMPLE IS REBUILT.

This is a date that there can be much certainty about, as the order for rebuilding the temple had not been given when this prophecy was made, and it would be an easy matter to learn the time Messiah should come when the order to rebuild the temple should be given. Dan. 9:25 gives us quite a definite clue as to when Messiah *must* be born. The prophecy reads as follows: "Know therefore and understand, that from the going forth of the commandment to restore and to build Jerusalem, unto the Messiah the Prince, shall be seven weeks, and three score and two weeks."

This is the most definite prophecy as to time that we have yet found, and one that can easily be comprehended. The "command to rebuild Jerusalem" had not been given when this was spoken, and certainly when it is given, the date can be fixed with almost absolute certainty. Daniel wrote this prophecy in the year B. C. 538, and the command to rebuild Jerusalem was given by Artaxerxes Longimanus, in the year 457 B. C. (See book of Ezra, chap. 7.) The weeks being understood to be weeks of years, as we find it in Num. 14:34, and Ezek. 4:6, "each day for a year," being the Bible's own way of interpreting itself, we find that there were seventy times seven, or four hundred and ninety years from the time of the going forth of the commandment to build the city of Jerusalem; these 490 years being added to the year B. C. 457, brings us to the year A. D. 33, the time when Jesus was cut off or crucified.

Again, we learn from Daniel that in the "Days of those kings, shall the God of heaven set up a kingdom, ... it shall break in pieces and consume these kingdoms, and it shall stand forever." Dan. 2:44.

We find in Luke 1:32, 33, concerning the prophecy of the angel as to the birth of Jesus: "He shall be great, and shall be called the 'Son of the Highest'; and the Lord shall give unto Him the throne of his father David: and He shall reign over the house of Jacob for ever; and of His kingdom there shall be no end." Here the prophecy made just before His birth agrees fully with Daniel's prophecy, made more than 600 years before the event took place. Tracing the promises step by step, we next come to the class of prophecies as to *where* He should be born.

3. PLACE OF HIS BIRTH.

As we go on in the investigation of these prophecies, we will be astonished sometimes, at the minute accuracy that God has pointed out the particulars as to the birth of Him who should redeem Israel; and here we have a careful naming of the very place where He must be born.

(1.) THE TOWN NAMED.

Micah, the Morasthite, who prophesied in the country of Judah, made a prophecy about the time of the death of Hezekiah, 710 B. C., as to where the coming Messiah should be born. His promise reads thus:

Micah 5:2: "But thou Beth-lehem Ephratah, though thou be little among the thousands of Judah, yet out of thee shall He come forth unto me that is to be ruler in Israel; whose goings forth have been from of old, from everlasting."

We need no more definite location where the Son of God should be born than this; and we must remember that this prophecy was made over 700 years before it was fulfilled.

(2.) THE TOWN WAS SO UNDERSTOOD.

The question may arise in the minds of some, "Is this sufficiently definite to enable the people to know where He must be born?" And we have only to turn to Matt. 2:1–6, to learn the facts in the case. From the report of the "chief priests and the scribes of the people" whom Herod called upon to know about the place where he should be born, we see that they made no hesitation in telling Herod that Messiah should be born in Bethlehem; and they quoted this very passage of Micah's as a sufficient proof that he *must* be born there. They made no delay upon the subject, but answered at *once*, as if that question had been well understood long ago, and that it was readily answered by all who had given the subject any thought.

Is it necessary to mention that Jesus was born in Bethlehem? Every one, who knows anything of the New Testament, knows also that Jesus was born in Bethlehem, as we are told by Matt. 2:1. So, also, Luke tells the same story, Luke 2:4–7. Here we find complete fulfillment as to the birth place of Jesus.

4. MANNER OF HIS BIRTH.

Certain things were told as to the way that Messiah was to be born into the world; and if these do not occur in the case of Jesus, He can not be the Messiah. Let us notice:

(1.) MESSIAH'S "SIGN."

There was a certain "sign" that was to attend the birth of Messiah, very extraordinary, and in fact, unprecedented, and yet it was to be *the "sign"* of the One who was to come to redeem the world. It is Isaiah who gives us this "sign," and he tells it as follows: Isa. 7:14: "Therefore the Lord himself shall give you a *sign;* Behold, a *virgin* shall conceive, and shall bear a Son, and shall call His name "*Immanuel.*"*

We shall not stop here to comment upon this name, to show that He was to be Divine; that will be noticed later on; but we shall notice some striking things that *must* occur, when the Messiah should make His appearance in the world. The "Sign" which God Himself gave, is one to which very many object, and they seriously complain of the way which God chose to bring His Son into the world. It is remarkably strange that God can not do things right and to the taste and notions of many of the sinners. If they were not sinners, what God does would be far more acceptable to them; and their objecting to the "sign," which God said should attend the coming of His Son into the world, only proves their sinful natures, but does not, in the least, destroy the fact that being born of a *virgin* was the God-chosen way for Messiah's birth. Had Jesus not been born of a *virgin*, He never could have laid a tenable claim to being the Messiah; for that very thing is the God-chosen "sign" by which

---

*This is a Hebrew name, made up of the words, "im" means "with;" "manu" means "Us;" and "el" a contraction of Elohim, a common word for "God." Immanuel means therefore, literally "With us God," or "God with us."

His Son should be known when He appeared. Whoever objects to this *virgin-birth* of the Lord Jesus, rejects the very "sign" by which He was to be identified. Let this be pondered well before He be rejected.

(2.) MESSIAH'S NAMES.

Besides the name given Him in the last paragraph, there were some other names by which He should be known, and they are quite remarkable. Isaiah speaks again, and tells us these names of the Great Coming Redeemer. Says he, Isa. 9:6: "For unto us a child is born, unto us a Son is given: and the government shall be upon His shoulder: and His name shall be called 'Wonderful Counsellor,' 'The mighty God,' 'The everlasting Father,' 'The Prince of Peace.'"

Notice the meanings of these names, and learn something from each. We learn some characteristic of the one to whom a name is given by divine authority. Practically, all the Bible names, and especially those given by the voice of God, have a striking meaning, and if we learn the meaning of the name, we shall also learn some characteristic of the one who bears the name.

"Abraham," father of a multitude; "Solomon," the man of peace; "Samuel," heard of God, and so on; so the names here given to the coming Messiah have each a remarkable meaning. The name "Messiah" means the One whom God has anointed; the same meaning is in the Greek word "Kristos," from which comes our word "Christ," all meaning the One whom God has anointed (to be king). So also He is called "Shiloh," because He is the Peaceful One. "My peace I leave with you," said He. The name "Yesuah," our word "Jesus," means "Savior"; and so these names given above reveal other characteristics to the wonderful Personage of the coming Messiah. "Peleh," translated "Wonderful," is quite an appropriate name for Him who is to have such a wonderful birth; in His matchless purity of His character; in the divine words which came from His lips; in His wonderful life, death and resurrection, as well as the wonderful influence His name has to this day over millions, indeed it is wonderful!! And the words "El Gibbor," translated "Mighty God," because He is mighty God indeed, "in whom dwells the fullness of the God-head bodily," Col. 2:9; and the name "Abhe Adh," translated "Everlasting Father," or as the Hebrew has it, "Father of Eternity;" though here a little babe born in Bethlehem, yet His goings forth are from everlasting; as He Himself said (John 8:58), "Before Abraham was, I am."

And the name "Sar Shalom," "The Prince of Peace" (see note, bottom page 19), shews the Messiah to be a man of peace, as the Lord Jesus Christ was in fact.*

---

*Here might be inserted the name in Psa. 2:12, the unusual word in Hebrew, except in poetry, " Bar," but a dispute is as to what it is from; some say it is from "bara," to create, but I believe it is from "barar," to choose, be chosen.

CHAPTER II.

MESSIAH'S RECEPTION IN THE WORLD.

1. THE MAGI TO VISIT HIM.

DAVID speaks in Psa. 72:10 on this wise, likely about Solomon and his riches, but in type of the Messiah, "The kings of Tarshish and of the isles of the sea shall bring presents: the kings of Seba and Sheba shall offer gifts." Again in v. 15, "And He shall live, and to Him shall be given the gold of Sheba: prayer shall be made for Him, and daily shall He be praised." Matt. 2:1,2, tells us of the praise that was offered to Jesus by the wise men from the East.

2. PERSECUTED AT BIRTH.

One would suppose that of all the visitors to this sin-cursed earth, He who was to free us from our sins, and bring us back into favor with God, would be the most welcome of all personages that could come to our world; but instead of being welcomed, He was to be so severely persecuted that it became a matter of prophecy, in the days of Jeremiah. He wrote in the time of the captivity, about the year 606 B. C., and following is what he says, Jer. 31:15: "Thus saith the Lord, A voice was heard in Ramah, lamentation and bitter weeping; Rahel weeping for her children, refused to be comforted for her children, because they were not." It is only necessary to call the attention of the reader to the passage found in Matt. 2:16–18, to show that Jesus was so persecuted; Herod, wanting to worship Him, as he feigned, asked the wise men to return and report where the child could be found; but he intended to kill Him instead of paying Him divine honors. Then it was that he sent soldiers to Bethlehem and had all the children murdered from two years old and under; and the passage in Matthew says that this was the fulfillment of the prophecy made by Jeremiah as to the weeping in Ramah: so this sad prophecy finds fulfillment in its sadder sequel.

3. WILL BE DRIVEN FROM HIS COUNTRY.

"He came unto His own and His own received Him not," is the comment which John makes upon the way that the Lord was welcomed, or rather not welcomed, by His people.

"He came to seek and to save that which was lost;" and the very lost ones whom He "came to seek and to save" are those who persecuted Him. Oh! the malice in the hearts of those who refuse to accept the Son of God: "Ye will not come unto me that ye might have life," says the patient Savior of lost men.

Says Hosea 11:1: "I . . . . loved Him, and called my Son out of Egypt." Why should He be obliged to call His Son out of a foreign country? It is on account of the malice of those to whom He came. Says Matt. 2:14, 15: "When he (Joseph) arose, he took the young child and His mother by night, and departed into Egypt; and was there until the death of Herod; that it might be fulfilled which was spoken of the Lord by the prophet saying, "Out of Egypt have I called my Son."

Egypt, the prison of the ancestors of the Jews, becomes the retreat and refuge and home of Him, who is come to save the Jews and all the rest of the world.

Is it not strange that fourteen and a half centuries after the Jews fled *from* Egypt that they might worship their God, here the Son of God must flee *to* Egypt to save His life from being taken by the Jews?

Jesus was kept in Egypt till the death of Herod, after which He was brought back to the land of Palestine, and was taken to Nazareth: that it might be fulfilled which was spoken by the prophets, "He shall be called a Nazarene." Matt. 2:23.

Here in this obscure town, did the Son of God "increase in wisdom and stature (or age) and the favor with God and man," till He passed the days of his childhood, boyhood, and early manhood. Here He worked at the humble calling of a carpenter; and He learned the first lessons of nature, which He was so fond of using in His matchless parables during His public life and ministry. It was also here that He first worshipped His Father in His early years, ever attending the synagogue, "as was His custom." And here both prophecy and history leave the Messiah till His public appearance, except His attendance of worship in Jerusalem, Luke 2:42-52. Luke adds that "He went down with them, and came to Nazareth, and was subject unto them: but His mother kept all these sayings in her heart. And Jesus increased in wisdom and stature (or age) and in favor with God and man."

CHAPTER III.

NATURES OF THE COMING MESSIAH.

THE ancestry of the coming Messiah is very carefully pointed out by the prophets in the Old Testament. While they do not tell us each individual who shall be in the line of His descent, yet so clearly is the line traced, that no fair minded person can be misled, or fail to see whence He *must* come. Let us notice how clearly the line is traced by the prophets.

1. HIS HUMAN NATURE: HIS NATURAL ANCESTRY.

There seems to be two periods chosen by the prophets in which men are named as the ancestors of Messiah, and those who are named in each group are father, son, etc.

(1.) HIS EARLIEST ANCESTRY NAMED.

Beginning as far back as the year 2000 B. C., or near that time, we find the first name in the list of His ancestors: we see that He will be

a. OF ABRAHAM'S SEED.

The very first promise of the Messiah's ancestry was recorded of Abraham, and that promise is repeated a number of times, no less than *five times* in the book of Genesis: chaps. 12:3; 18:18; 22:18; 26:4; and 28:14.

We will not quote all of them, but as a sample of these promises, let us take Gen. 22:18: "And in thy (Abraham) seed shall all the nations be blessed; because thou hast obeyed my voice." The same thought is in all the other passages named; as the promises advance, they grow in definiteness. Abraham was the father of several sons (Gen. 25:1–7) but the prophecies narrow the line to very particular limits, as we shall notice in the following:

b. TO BE OF THE SEED OF ISAAC.

In Gen. 21:12, the promise is given to Isaac to be one of the ancestors of the Messiah; for it says, "For in Isaac shall thy seed be called."

Paul positively says that this refers to Messiah (Christ) in Gal. 3:16. He says, "Now to Abraham and his seed were the promises made. He saith not, 'And to seeds,' as of many; but as of One, 'And to *thy seed*,' which is Christ"

(Messiah). Tracing the line of ancestry of Messiah, the next named is

c. HE IS TO BE OF THE LINE OF JACOB.

In the books of Moses we find two very clear prophecies that Messiah shall be of the seed of Jacob. Num. 24:17: "I shall see Him, but not now: I shall behold Him, but not nigh: there shall come a Star out of Jacob, and a Sceptre shall rise out of Israel." And then, v. 19: "Out of Jacob shall come He that shall have dominion." Of the sons of Isaac, Esau is rejected, and Jacob chosen to be the son through whom the Messiah is to come.

These prophecies are as sign-boards to point to Him who was promised; and they are given that we as well, may also know Him. How carefully does God mark the line! With what accuracy does he point out the very footsteps of His coming Son!

d. TO BE OF THE LINE OF JUDAH.

The promises are not quite as clear that Judah is in the line of Messiah's ancestry, but sufficiently explicit as to leave but little doubt that he is one of the line. We shall notice two prophecies that do not mention the name of Judah, but the third does name him. Says

Moses in Deut. 18:15: "The Lord thy God will raise up unto thee a Prophet from the midst of thee, of thy brethren, like unto me; unto Him ye shall hearken." And in v. 18 of the same chapter, he says, using the words of God himself: "I will raise them up a Prophet from among their brethren, like unto thee (Moses), and will put my words in his mouth; and he shall speak unto them all that I shall command Him." But the following is a little more specific as to Judah being in the line of Messiah's ancestry. Gen. 49:10: "The sceptre shall not depart from Judah, nor a lawgiver from between his feet, until *Shiloh** come; and unto Him shall the gathering of the people be."

With Judah ends, for many years, the naming of those who are to be the ancestors of Messiah; there is a period of over *five hundred years*, in which there is no one named; not till we come to the days of Jesse. Here we have but two names given clearly, though we might claim the name of Solomon; still there may be a little reasonable doubt about his name; we will mention then,

(2.) HIS LATTER ANCESTRY.

Leaving blank the intervening names who should be in the line, and not taking into the

---

* See note, page 19.

account the historical statement about the ancestry of Jesse, given in Ruth, chap. 4, we come to the direct prophecies.

a. HE IS TO BE OF THE SEED OF JESSE.

Isa. 11:1: "And there shall come forth a rod out of the stem of Jesse, and a Branch shall grow out of his roots." v. 10: "And in that day there shall be a root of Jesse, which shall stand for an ensign of the people; to it shall the Gentiles seek."

And now we come to the last name mentioned in the line.

b. OF THE SEED OF DAVID.

Says Psa. 89:3,4: "I have made a covenant with my chosen, I have sworn unto David my servant, Thy seed will I establish forever, and build up thy throne to all generations." Also vv. 29 and 36. Jeremiah also mentions David as in the line of Messiah's progenitors, Jer. 23:5,6: "Behold the days come, saith the Lord, that I will raise unto David, a Righteous Branch, and a King shall reign and prosper, and shall execute judgment and justice in the earth. In His day shall Judah be saved, and Israel shall dwell safely; and this is His name, THE LORD, OUR RIGHTEOUSNESS." So, again

Jer. 33:15 says of the Messiah's coming in the line of David: "In those days, and at that time, will I cause the Branch of Righteousness to grow up unto David: and He shall execute judgment and righteousness in the land."

These last prophecies can not have referred to David or Solomon in person; for they had been dead many years when Jeremiah wrote these words; it must refer to the Messiah.

With this closes the prophecies as to the particular line of ancestry in which Messiah *must* come; we refer to the accounts of Matthew and Luke as to the ancestry of the Lord Jesus Christ. Turning to these accounts, we see that both Matthew and Luke give these very identical names as in the line of ancestry of which Jesus was born. Every name is mentioned in the two accounts, and not in the same order, but in a reversed order, Matthew beginning with Abraham and coming on down to Jesus, while Luke begins with Jesus and goes back to Abraham, and in fact, to Adam; yet all the names are in both; Abraham, Isaac, Jacob, Judah, and then the names in between, and then Jesse and David. Certainly here is a remarkable fulfillment in the case of Jesus of Nazareth, as to the line of His birth.

2. HIS DIVINE NATURE: HIS DIVINITY.

And now we approach the greatest mystery of the Messiah: that He is to be both human and divine! Partaking of the nature of both, and combining in Himself both God and man! This is, and was, and is likely to remain, the greatest mystery connected with the God-man, who was to save the world from sin. While the prophecies are not so numerous as on some other points connected with the Messiah, yet they are very definite. Difficult as the two natures of the Messiah are to be understood, human and divine combined, yet it was clearly foretold that Messiah *must* have just such a compound nature.

And then think of it, dear reader, how else could it have been? Had He come, a mere man, even though perfectly holy and sinless, what could He have done towards saving men? His death would have had no merit in it more than was necessary for Himself as a man, and could have done no one else one particle of good; it would have been but the death of a good man, and that is all; and if He had come as God, altogether in His divine nature, He could have had no crucifiable nature, so to speak; no nature that *could* have suffered for lost sinners; therefore the Redeemer *had* to come, in the very nature of things, as a God-man, combining the natures of both, that He might reconcile the two together. Those who deny His humanity, would totally unfit Him from being available to do the work that a Redeemer *must* do; and on the other hand, those who deny His divinity also deny to Him that essential holiness and meritorious value that *must* be in the Redeemer of lost men; but Jesus, fathered by divinity and mothered by humanity, unites and combines in the One being all the essential qualifications that are absolutely indispensable in the Redeemer of sinful humanity.

So much for that question; and now let us look at what the prophets said Messiah would be.

Isaiah and Jeremiah tell us about this two-fold nature. They lived six or seven centuries before the year of our Lord. Isaiah wrote about a hundred years before the "Babylonish Captivity," in the land of Judah, about 760 B. C., when he began, and closed about 700 B. C. Jeremiah wrote during the captivity, beginning some years before it, and closing during that period. Notice then, first, Isa. 9:6: "For unto us a child is born, unto us a son is given : and the government shall be upon his shoulder: and his name shall be called Wonderful Counsellor, The mighty God, The everlasting Father, The Prince of Peace." Divinity is too plainly seen here to need any comment, but it is even clearer, if possible, in the next passage quoted.

Isa. 25:9: "And it shall be said in that day, Lo, this is our God: we have waited for Him; and he will save us : this is the Lord ; we have waited for Him, we will be glad and rejoice in His salvation." Here it is plainly stated that He is to be divine ; He is "Our God."

Jeremiah is as clear as to his divinity when he says, "Behold the days come, saith the Lord, that I will raise unto David a Righteous Branch, and a King shall reign and prosper, and shall execute judgment and justice in the earth. In His days shall Judah be saved, and Israel shall dwell in safety: and this is His name, THE LORD OUR RIGHTEOUSNESS." Jer. 23:5,6.

That Jesus fulfilled all these prophecies we have but to turn to the first chapter of John, in which he says he did fulfill them. Says John,

1:1–3: "In the beginning was the Word, and the Word was with God, and the Word was God. The same was in the beginning with God. All things were made by him; and without him was not any thing made that was made."

And so the whole chapter goes on to show that Jesus was a divine being, as the prophets said Messiah would be.

Paul asserts the same about Jesus, Phil. 2:6: "Who, being in the form of God, thought it not robbery to be equal with God." So Jesus said it of himself to the woman at the well of Jacob, John 4:26. Also John 10:30: "I and my Father are one." So John 17:22: "That they may be one as *we are one*," (i. e. God and Jesus).

The divinity of Jesus is one of the leading and foremost doctrines of the whole New Testament, more written of by John than any one else, as that was one of the leading features of his Gospel; but mentioned by nearly every one of the New Testament writers, and dwelt upon by all as the hope of the Christian and the foundation of the entire structure of the Christian religion. Strange as the two-fold nature of the Christ was then and is yet, they seemed to rest everything upon this fact.

Wonderful as the Messiah was to be, we find that the man Christ Jesus was just as remarkable; just as incomprehensible in his two-fold nature; combined the same natures, human and divine, that it was foretold by the prophets Messiah would have.

Does not the babe of Bethlehem fulfill these prophecies?

CHAPTER IV.

MESSIAH AND HIS DOCTRINES.

AS the prophecies approach nearer the time for Messiah to come, they become more numerous, clearer, and more minute. We will now notice some characteristics both of the Messiah Himself as well as His doctrines which He shall advance.

1. MESSIAH'S GENTLENESS.

We are not left in doubt as to the disposition of Messiah, but He is fully pictured by the prophets. Oh! how God did prepare the world for the recognition of His Messiah when He should come, but how poorly they did recognize Him, and how slow they were to accept Him; and many are just as slow to accept Him now. Often do they tell us what He is to be, and right well, indeed, do they picture the Man Jesus the Nazarene. Let us observe that they tell us He will be,

(1.) AS A TENDER SHEPHERD.

Says Isa. 40:11: "He shall feed his flock like a shepherd: he shall gather the lambs in his arms, and carry them in his bosom." What a beautiful picture this is of the tender care Messiah will have for His own. Such gentle love, such true devotion to those who are His redeemed. And also says Ezek. 34:23: "And I will set up one Shepherd over them, and he shall feed them, even my servant David;* he shall feed them, and he shall be their shepherd."

How fittingly the verse comes to mind, Psa. 23:1: "The Lord is my shepherd; I shall not want." But when we come to look at the fulfillment of these passages and others, He becomes still more gentle and tender towards the redeemed. John tells us much of the "Good Shepherd" in his Gospel. See the words of Jesus Himself, "I am the Good Shepherd: The Good Shepherd giveth his life for the sheep." So tender is His love, so much is He interested in the sheep that He even lays down his own life for them that they may not perish,

---

*This can not refer to David personally, for he had been dead more than *five hundred years* when this was written. It must therefore refer to the Great Representative of the throne of David, even the Messiah Himself.

but be safe. Paul says of Him, Heb. 13:20: "Now the God of peace, that brought again from the dead our Lord Jesus, that Great Shepherd of the sheep, through the blood of the everlasting covenant." So in Peter 2:25, we find additional testimony as to His being the Great Shepherd who was to come: "For ye were as sheep going astray; but are now returned unto the Shepherd and Bishop of your souls." Other passages can be found to the same point; for instance, in the tenth of John, several passages are recorded: v. 7, "I am the door of the sheep;" v. 14, "I am the Good Shepherd;" v. 16, "Other sheep have I;" v. 26, "But ye (Jews) believe not, because ye are not my sheep;" v. 27, "My sheep hear my voice, and I know them, and they follow me;" and nearly the whole chapter is a figure of Jesus being the Shepherd of the sheep, as the prophets said Messiah would be.

(2.) A MAN OF MEEKNESS.

Messiah was never to be a noisy man in the streets, but would be a man of peculiar meekness, as we see from the two following passages: Isa. 42:2,3, "He shall not cry, nor lift up, nor cause his voice to be heard in the street.

A bruised reed shall he not break, and the smoking flax shall he not quench." And the passage in Zechariah, as to His entering Jerusalem, he also mentions how lowly He will be.

Zech. 9:9, "Behold, thy King cometh unto thee: he is just, and having salvation; lowly, and riding upon an ass."

Certainly the one who can fulfill all these conditions must be a man of remarkable character; one who shall possess more than the usual amount of patience and gentleness.

Let us see how Jesus fulfills them.

Matthew 12:19, says the action there mentioned was done that it might be fulfilled which was spoken by the prophet Esaias: "He shall not cry; neither shall any man hear his voice in the streets. A bruised reed shall he not break, and smoking flax shall he not quench." This is very pointed and direct testimony to the gentleness of Jesus, and we find the same writer continues, 21:4,5: "All this was done, that it might be fulfilled which was spoken by the prophet, saying, Tell ye the daughter of Sion, Behold, thy King cometh to thee, meek, and sitting upon an ass." The gentleness of Jesus is one of the most striking, as well as one of the greatest characteristics of His wonderful life. His was a life of love and tenderness, of "going about doing good," and never was He seen noisy in the streets, or in any way boisterous. He was as quiet as a woman, though never effeminate; as tender as a nursing mother, yet never unmanly; surely this man answers to the full description of Messiah's meekness.

(3.) HE WILL BE WELL-PLEASING TO GOD.

Says Isa. 42:1: "Behold my servant, whom I uphold; mine elect, in whom my soul delighteth; I have put my Spirit upon him: he shall bring forth judgment to the Gentiles." More than once do we hear the voice of God, in the New Testament, calling Jesus His beloved. Says God, in Matt. 3:17: "This is my beloved Son, in whom I am well pleased." Again, Matt. 12:17,18: "That it might be fulfilled which was spoken by Isaiah the prophet, saying, Behold my servant, whom I have chosen; my beloved, in whom my soul is well pleased." And still again, Matt. 17:5: "This is my beloved Son, in whom I am well pleased; hear ye him."

God was remarkably well pleased with Jesus: why are not you, dear reader, well pleased with him also?

Certainly no one can ask for a less holy Savior than Jesus was; for of what use to the world could a Savior be that was not absolutely holy? He could be of no more use than any other man. And then on the other hand, a more holy Savior can not be demanded than Jesus was; for He was without sin at all; more holiness He could not have; less holiness would render him unfit to be a Savior at all; therefore was God well pleased with Him; why will you not be also well pleased with this Son of God?

2. HE WILL BE PATIENT UNDER ALL TRIALS.

This is one of the strange characteristics of Messiah. When the Jews read that He was to be a great conqueror, as they could easily learn from the prophecies about him, and also saw that He was to be very meek and humble under all trials, they could not comprehend how these two apparently contradictory characteristics could be united in one and the same person; and therefore, they believed that there were to be two Messiahs; one a great conqueror, and the other an humble, meek man, patient under all trials. They failed to understand how so great a conqueror as Messiah was to be could also be the humble, meek "Man of Sorrow" that the prophecies said Messiah should be.

(1.) HE WILL BE SORELY MALTREATED.

As to the maltreatment which Messiah should endure, we have more than one passage to testify. Notice how minute. Isa. 50:6: "I gave my back to the smiters, and my cheeks to them that plucked off the hair: I hid not my face from shame and spitting." In the very same tone do we find Jeremiah, in the Lamentations, 3:30, foretelling Messiah's maltreatment: "He giveth his cheek to him that smiteth him: he is filled full with reproach."

How strangely this must have sounded to the proud Jews, who were looking for, and especially wanting a haughty potentate to be their deliverer.

Consulting the testimony in regard to Jesus, let us see how his maltreatment coincides with that which these prophecies foretold of Messiah's.

All the four writers of the Gospel come in as witnesses. Take them in the order that they appear in the New Testament: Matt. 26:67, 68: "Then did they spit in his face, and buffeted him; and others smote him with the palms of their hands, saying, Prophesy unto us, thou Christ, Who is he that smote thee?" And again the same in Matt. 27:30: "And they spit upon him, and took the reed, and smote him on the head." Mark uses almost the same words as Matthew, in giving his evidence. Mark 14:65: "And some began to spit on him, and to cover his face, and to buffet him, and to say unto him, Prophesy: and the servants did strike him with the palms of their hands."

Luke tells the same story, but modifies the words, 22:63, 64: "And the men that held Jesus mocked him, and smote him. And when they had blindfolded him, they struck him on the face, and asked him, saying, Prophesy, who is it that smote thee?"

Not only did Jesus endure these indignities, but even greater ones. Mark 15:15: "And so Pilate, willing to content the people, released Barabbas unto them, and delivered Jesus, *when he had scourged him.*" So Matt., 27:26: "And when he had scourged Jesus." And also says John, 19:1: "Then Pilate therefore took Jesus, and scourged him." And so continued the brutal treatment as long as they wished to abuse him. When we remember what a Roman scourging was, we can better understand how severe the maltreatment was which the Messiah should receive, and the treatment that Jesus did endure was identical with it.

It might be well to stop and ask what the prophets say the Messiah should do, under all these trials and indignities.

(2.) HE WILL BE SILENT, WHEN AFFLICTED.

Humanly speaking, it would seem that if the great Son of the living God should be so treated as the prophets said he would, the very heavens would come down to avenge his wrongs.

Turn to Isa. 53:7, where we are told what the Messiah would do, when grossly abused. "He was oppressed, and he was afflicted, yet he opened not his mouth: he is brought as a lamb to the slaughter, and as a sheep before her shearers is dumb, so he openeth not his mouth." Let us see the very remarkable manner in which Jesus fulfilled all these things: Matt. 26:62,63: "And the high priest arose, and said unto him, Answerest thou nothing? what is it which these witness against thee? But Jesus held his peace." So again in Matt. 27:12–14: "And when he was accused of the chief priests and elders, he answered nothing. Then said

Pilate unto him, Hearest thou not how many things they witness against thee? And he answered him to never a word: insomuch that the governor marvelled greatly." Does not Jesus here fulfill the prophecies concerning Messiah?

(3.) WILL PRAY FOR HIS ENEMIES.

And what further did the prophets say Messiah would do, under all these trials? We have learned that he would be silent, and that Jesus was remarkably silent, so that even Pilate marvelled greatly; but there are some other things that Messiah would do also. He would pray for those who maltreated him. We will see if Jesus did this.

Psa. 109:4: "For my love they are my adversaries: but I give myself unto prayer." That is to say, because Messiah loved the people whom He came to save, they were His *adversaries!* Very strange statement indeed! When we love people, and want to do them good, then it is that they ought to treat us, at least, civilly; but not so with the Messiah: it was because He did love them, and wanted to do them good by saving their souls from sin, is the reason given why they hated him. It is the same to-day, and has been, all the days since man became a sinner; hating Him who wants to benefit you by taking you away from your sins. Look at what Jesus did, and compare it with what Messiah was to do, and learn how they correspond.

Luke 23:34: "Then said Jesus, Father, forgive them; for they know not what they do." Praying for his tormentors, while they were tormenting him the most severely! Does not Jesus here fulfill the prophecy? Says Paul, Rom. 8:34: "Who is he that condemneth? It is Christ that died, yea rather, that is risen again, who is even at the right hand of God, who also maketh intercession for us."

A persecuted, patient intercessor for sinners, Messiah was to be: Jesus *was* a patient, persecuted intercessor for sinners. In reason, does not Jesus here fulfill the prophecies concerning Messiah?

Jesus still is at the right hand of the Father to make intercession for every one, who will repent of his sins and turn to God for pardon. It is one of the leading doctrines of the New Testament that Jesus is the intercessor for sinners, just as it is prophesied that Messiah should be. He is ready to intercede for you, dear reader, if you will turn to Him in repentance.

Will you not give Him that heart of thine?

3. MESSIAH'S DOCTRINES.

Never had there been a kingdom in the world which had not been ruled by the power of might and prowess of the king; but when the kingdom of the Messiah is to be set up, it shall be one that shall have altogether a different mode of government. Instead of the sword and spear or our modern firearms as the sceptre by which His kingdom should be ruled, Messiah should introduce a very different way of governing his kingdom: one of righteousness and love by which he should move his followers to obedience, as well as to win others to his kingdom. Such a thing had never been heard of, and was never attempted except by the Lord Jesus Christ. Notice

(1.) HIS SCEPTRE TO BE ONE OF LOVE AND RIGHTEOUSNESS.

In David's Psalm the 45th, vv. 6, 7, we find these words, in reference to Messiah's rule:

"Thy throne, O God, is for ever and ever: the sceptre of thy kingdom is a right sceptre. Thou lovest righteousness, and hatest wickedness: therefore God, thy God, hath anointed thee with the oil of gladness above thy fellows."

Let him who comes claiming to be the Messiah, attempt to rule his kingdom by other means than by the love here expressed, and he can have no claim whatever, to being the Messiah of prophecy. How was it with the Lord Jesus? Heb. 1:8, tells us that this very quotation was fulfilled in the Lord Jesus.

Again in John 13:34: Jesus says "A new commandment I give unto you, That ye love one another; as I have loved you, that ye also love one another." And in eleven other places can we find this same thought expressed as to the "new" commandment of loving one another. John 15:12: "This is my commandment, That ye love one another, as I have loved you." And so might all the other passages be found in the same line. This is indeed a "new" commandment; they had heard the old commandments in the decalogue: but here is a "new" one which Jesus brings into the world. Personal love, not only between God and man, but personal love between man and man. The kingdom of Jesus would knit all mankind into a great family of loving brotherhood, did all mankind accept His teachings, and become converted by the power of the Holy Spirit.

(2.) REGENERATION PROMISED.

We read from Jer. 31:33, the promise of the remarkable doctrine of being "born again." "But this shall be the covenant that I will make with the house of Israel: After those days, saith the Lord, I will put my law in their inward parts, and write it in their hearts; and will be their God, and they shall be my people." So do we find the same thought repeated in the very next chapter, in these words, Jer. 32:39: "And I will give them one heart, and one way, that they fear me for ever." Also Ezek. 36:26, testifies to the same idea with a little variation of words, thus: "And a new heart also will I give you." Certainly the meaning that is to be here learned is that an inward remodeling of the sinner is to take place, and that God is to be the author of that change, as is seen by the expression, "Writing His law in their hearts," and "giving a new heart," etc. This strange doctrine was never taught till we hear it from the sacred lips of the Lord Jesus, as he taught it to Nicodemus, John 3:3:

"Verily, verily, I say unto thee, Except a man (any one) be born again, he cannot see the kingdom of God." And v. 7: "Marvel not that I said unto thee, Ye must be born again." Such a new teaching was too new for Nicodemus to comprehend; and he asked a foolish question, showing that he had no idea as to what it really meant? but Jesus told him the absolute necessity of having a new nature, before one can hope to enjoy the blessings of heaven. Based upon the teachings of the Savior, the New Testament writers say much concerning the same doctrine. Paul in II. Cor. 5:17: "If any man be in Christ, he is a new creature; old things are passed away; behold, all things are become new." This teaching is plain, that to enter the kingdom of heaven, one *must* have a renewed nature, and the change *must* be made by the God who created man; and not until then is he at all ready to enjoy the presence of God, having the same nature with God.

How could man enjoy being with God, and yet have a sinful nature? Paul's passage in Rom. 8:16,17, fits well here: "The Spirit itself beareth witness with our spirit, that we are the children of God: And if children, then heirs; heirs of God, and joint heirs with Christ."

There was also another promise which was to be fulfilled when the Messiah came, a thing that was never heard of before, in the world's history; and that was,

(3.) THE PROMISED ABIDING PRESENCE OF THE HOLY SPIRIT.

This was as new to the world as was the promise of the renewed nature, or Regeneration, but none the less clearly promised.

Ezek. 11:19: Says God, "I will put a *new* spirit within you; and I will take the stony heart out of their flesh." And so he repeats the same promise in a later chapter, Ezek. 36:26,27: "And a *new* spirit will I put within you: and cause you to walk in my statutes, and ye shall keep my judgments, and do them." This new and strange doctrine had its fulfillment after the Lord Jesus came and went. He promised the Spirit a number of times, mostly recorded by John. For instance, John 16:7: "It is expedient for you that I go away; for if I go not away, the Comforter will not come unto you; but if I depart, I will send him unto you." Also in 15:26: "But when the Comforter is come, whom I will send unto you from the Father." And so other passages: turning to the book of Acts 2:1,4, we may learn what was meant by "sending the Comforter," for it reads, "And when the day of Pentecost was fully come, . . . they were all filled with the Holy Ghost, and began to speak," etc.

Notice, or you may fail to see the point in full. God had promised to send the Holy Spirit *when* the Messiah should come: and not until He did come, need any one expect that the Holy Spirit should come; but when the Lord Jesus had come and gone back to heaven, it was then, and not until then that the Holy Spirit came to fulfill the promise. What must be the unavoidable conclusion, then dear reader? Certainly there can be but one conclusion, and that is, this same Jesus *must* be the promised Messiah. Certainly the dullest mind can see that Jesus *must* be the Messiah; for he fulfills the prophecies about Messiah; then Jesus and Messiah are one and the same person, *quod demonstandum est.*

CHAPTER V.

MESSIAH'S LIFE AND LABORS.

WE now come to consider the commencement of the work Messiah was to do in the world; how it shall begin, together with the account of the man who was to usher in the early stages of the Messiah's earthly labors, and apprize the world that Messiah was at hand. Let us notice then,

1. THE BEGINNING OF HIS KINGDOM.

Messiah should not appear in the world unheralded, but He should have some one to go before Him to announce His arrival; so we will now listen to

(1.) THE FORERUNNER.

We have three distinct prophecies that there is to be a forerunner, whose duty it is to warn the people to prepare for His coming, and to apprize the world generally that the day of Messiah is at hand. It was John the Baptist, who came to tell the people that the Messiah was near, even at hand, and that they should repent and turn to this Messiah.

(2.) THE WILDERNESS CRY.

The first prophecy was made over seven hundred years before the coming of the Lord Jesus, and the two later were made about four hundred years before His coming.

Says Isa. 40:3: "The voice of him that crieth in the wilderness, Prepare ye the way of the Lord, make straight in the desert a highway for our God." John the Baptist came in the wilderness of Judea, "in the fifteenth year of the reign of Tiberius Cesar, Pontius Pilate being the governor of Judea," Luke 3:1, and created quite an excitement throughout the whole country; insomuch that the Jews sent the priests from Jerusalem to inquire of him who he was: and his answer was, John 1:23, "I am the voice of one crying in the wilderness, Make straight the way of the Lord, as said the prophet Isaias." Matthew, Mark and Luke give similar accounts of John and his work. John the Baptist, though a very modest man, laid full claim to being the one sent to make this cry in the wilderness.

(3.) THE WAY PREPARED.

Malachi the last prophet who wrote in the Old Testament, ch. 3:1, says: "Behold, I will send my messenger, and he shall prepare the way before me." And the very last thing that is said in the Old Testament is that the Messiah should come, and that there should be a messenger to prepare the way for Him.

Mal. 4:5,6: "Behold, I will send you Elijah the prophet before the coming of the great and dreadful day of the Lord. And he shall turn the heart of the fathers to the children, and the heart of the children to their fathers, lest I come and smite the earth with a curse." And thus closes the Old Testament.

From these passages just quoted, it is beyond doubt that there was to come some one to prepare the way for the Messiah. Every one of the four evangelists, Matthew, Mark, Luke and John, says that John the Baptist was sent to prepare the way of the Lord.

We are not left to their testimony alone, though it ought to be sufficient of itself, to any honest minded man; but we have the testimony of Josephus, a Jewish historian, who lived near that time, and was well acquainted with the facts in the case; and he, though not a follower of the Lord Jesus at all, testifies to the following:

Josephus Antiq., b. 18, ch. 5, § 2: "Now some of the Jews thought that the destruction of Herod's army (in the battle with Aretas, king of Arabia,) came from God; and that very justly, as a punishment of what he did against John, who was called the Baptist: for he slew him, who was a good man and commanded the Jews to exercise virtue; both as to righteousness towards one another, and piety towards God, and so come to baptism. For that the washing in water would be acceptable to Him, if they made use of it, not in order to putting away or the remission of some sins only, but for the purification of the body; supposing still the soul was thoroughly purified beforehand by righteousness. Now when many came in crowds around him . . . Herod . . . thought it best by putting him to death, to prevent any mischief he might cause: accordingly he was sent a prisoner, out of Herod's suspicious temper, to Machaerus, the castle I before mentioned; and there was put to death." This is the testimony of one who was an enemy of the Lord Jesus, or at least, not a follower of his, and he can not therefore be accused of being prejudiced in his favor.

Jesus joins his testimony that John was his forerunner. Mark 9:13.

When Jesus himself was asked about the coming of Elijah, in the passage last quoted, as well as in Matt. 17:12,13, He said: "But I say unto you, That Elias is come already, and they knew him not, but have done unto him whatsoever they listed. Likewise shall also the Son of man suffer of them. Then the disciples understood that he spake unto them of John the Baptist." Here we have the combined testimony of both John and Jesus that John was the forerunner who was to come before the Messiah should appear in the world. If this claim of John the Baptist has ever been disputed that he was not the forerunner of the Messiah, it has not been my privilege to see or hear of it. Is there any more testimony needed to establish the fact that John the Baptist preacher of the desert was the forerunner of the Messiah prophesied of by the prophets? "In the mouth of two or three witnesses shall every word be established," II. Cor. 13:1. But we have the double of the two witnesses. A man was put to death by *two* witnesses, according to the law, as we may find in Deut. 17:6, and any of our courts of criminal law will, with the concurrent testimony of two witnesses, put a man to death now, if his crime so merit. Why not then rest assured that it is fully established that *John the Baptist preacher of the desert was the forerunner of the Messiah?*

Let us remember, however, that although the evidence of John's being the forerunner of the Messiah is so clear, and so conclusive, that it seems useless to attempt to deny it for a moment, yet when we acknowledge that he was such forerunner, we also must acknowledge that Jesus was the Messiah; for John never witness to any one whatever as being the Messiah, except to Jesus. John's office being established, then the claims of Jesus are just as surely established; for he said that Jesus was the "lamb of God that taketh away the sins of the world," John 1:29; and his whole life was given to nothing, absolutely nothing else than to testify that Jesus the Nazarene was the promised Messiah. John the Baptist was the forerunner of both the Messiah and Jesus; then Jesus is the promised Messiah, and the object of this book has been accomplished; but we have so much more proof and just as unanswerable as the above. Notice next,

2. MESSIAH TO BE A PREACHER OF THE GOSPEL.

One of the strongest characteristics of the coming Messiah was that He would be a preacher of the Gospel, or "Good News," as the word means. When He should come, what other men had tried to learn, He would teach. The peace that other men sought after, He would give to his followers. The class that other wise men ignored He would preach the Gospel to, and elevate them, and the downtrodden whom other teachers neglected, He would exalt to become the "Sons of God." And strangest of all (strange then), the bitterest enemies God had on earth would have the Gospel preached to them, and from them would the kingdom, which He came to establish, be made. Paul is a good example of this kind, and many thousands of others like him.

Notice some of the peculiarities of Messiah's preaching. Isaiah 61:1,2, tells us the following beautiful description of the preaching of the coming Messiah: "The Spirit of the Lord God is upon me; because the Lord hath anointed*

---

*The same word that is here translated "Anointed," the Hebrew word, "mashakh," is the same word from which the name "Messiah" is derived. The Hebrew form of Messiah is "Mashieah," and means "The Anointed;" as does the Greek translation, "Kristos," from which comes our word, "Christ." Jesus then is the Anointed One of God, He being the Messiah.

me to preach good tidings unto the meek; he hath sent me to bind up the brokenhearted, to proclaim liberty to the captives, and the opening of the prison to them that are bound; To proclaim the acceptable year of the Lord, and the day of vengeance of our God; to comfort all that mourn."

Such was the important duty of Him who was to be the Lord's Anointed. Hope may arise now to those who were bound down in sin, and to those who are captives of lust and iniquity.

Whenever this Messiah shall come to this sin-cursed world, then may there be rejoicing, such as had never been seen since Adam first walked the forbidden paths of sin.

Messiah should be a preacher of "good tidings"* to the world. How did Jesus fulfill this prophecy? Let us see.

One day, Jesus came to Nazareth, he went to church "as was his custom," and this being his old home, where he had been brought up, everybody knew him, according to the flesh, but not according to his real nature; and that day, they called upon him to talk to the people.

---

*Apropos to this point, i.e., that Messiah should be a preacher of the Gospel, is the observation that the word here translated, "To preach good tidings," is the word (Hebrew Basar, but here the Piel is used Bassare) which the LXX. uses in the Old Testament, the Greek word, "euaggelisasthai," aor. inf., meaning to preach the Gospel.

The minister handed him the roll of the prophets, and Jesus found the place (Isa. 61:1) where it is written, "The Spirit of the Lord is upon me;" and he began to read, and a strange fascination seized the people, why, they knew not, but they were spellbound, as it were, as he read the passage. What drew them to him? They had read and heard it read no doubt, often before. It could not be the newness of the passage that held them; but yet the "eyes of all of them that were in the synagogue were fastened upon him," as he began to tell them, "This day is this Scripture fulfilled in your ears," and so completely taken were they that "all bare him witness, and wondered at the gracious words which proceeded out of his mouth." Luke 4:16-22. Listen to him!

"Because he hath anointed me to preach the gospel to the poor;" and so he read the whole passage, and handed the roll back to the minister, and sat down (the way speakers usually addressed the people in those days), and astounded everybody by telling them that "This day is this Scripture fulfilled in your ears." Oh! will not the people make the welkin ring with their joyous shouts of ecstasy that the long expected One has come at last?

He whom the world has been needing so much and so long, will they not give him a great and glorious welcome? But no; if they do, it will not be in accord with the way Messiah was to be treated. (See Sec. 6, this chap. below.) He was to be "despised and rejected of men," and so verses 28, 29, Luke 4, tells the result.

"And all they in the synagogue . . . rose up, and thrust him out of the city, and led him unto the brow of the hill whereon their city was built, that they might cast him down headlong." Yea, surely, he is "despised and rejected of men."

Jesus himself refers to these prophecies, as proof of what and who he is, when John sent to him to know. Matt. 11:5,6: "If he (Jesus) was the One that was to come, or look we for another?" And the answer that Jesus sent back is well worthy of our careful consideration. He did not answer John and say, "Yes, I am the Messiah that was to come into the world;" but he referred him to the prophecies that were spoken about Messiah, just as he no doubt would do to-day, if he were asked the same question. When John Baptist asked him, Jesus sent word to him, "The blind receive their sight, the lame walk, the lepers are cleansed, the deaf hear, the dead are raised up, and the *poor have the gospel preached to them.*" As much as to say to John, "The blind see, just as it was foretold that they would, when Messiah came; the lame walk, just as it was prophesied that they would when Messiah came; the lepers are cleansed, just as it was predicted that they would be when Messiah should come; the deaf hear, the dead are raised up, and the poor have the gospel preached to them, just as it was foretold that it would be, when Messiah should come; therefore John, if I do the very things that Messiah was to do, can it be possible that you or any one else can fail to see and *know* that I *must* be the Messiah?" Such logic is irresistible and unanswerable.

3. TO BE A GREAT LIGHT.

Isaiah, in 49:6, tells us that the Messiah is to be a Great Light to the Gentiles. Notice how it reads:

"I will also give thee for a light to the Gentiles, that thou mayest be my salvation unto the end of the earth." And so Isa. 9:2: "The people that sat in darkness have seen a great Light; they that dwell in the land of the shadow of death, upon them hath the Light shined." And so again, Isa. 42:6: "I the Lord have called thee in righteousness and will hold thy hand, and will keep thee for a covenant of the people, for a Light of the Gentiles."

Says John 1:7,8: "The same (John the Baptist) came for a witness, to bear witness of the Light . . . that was the true Light." And again, John 4:14-16: "That it might be fulfilled which was spoken by Esaias the prophet, saying, The land of Zebulon, and the land of Nephthalim, by the way of the sea, beyond Jordon, Gallilee of the Gentiles; the people which sat in darkness saw a great Light, and to them which sat in the region and shadow of death, Light is sprung up." Thus do we see that Jesus fulfilled this very prophecy, as the Gospel writers say he did. He is indeed "the Light that lighteth every man that cometh into the world," as John says, 1:9.

4. MESSIAH TO BE A HEALER OF THE AFFLICTED.

Very clear and pointed are the passages which say that Messiah will be a great Healer. It is said in many places. Isa. 29:18,19: "And in that day shall the deaf hear the words of the book, and the eyes of the blind shall see out of obscurity, and out of darkness. The meek shall also increase their joy in the Lord, and the poor among men shall rejoice in the Holy One of Israel." But even plainer is the passage found in Isa. 35:5,6: "Then the eyes of the blind shall be opened, and the ears of the deaf shall be unstopped. Then shall the lame man leap as a hart, and the tongue of the dumb sing: for in the wilderness shall waters break out, and streams in the desert."

If the one who shall claim to be the Messiah can not and does not heal the afflicted, He can not lay any tenable claim to his being the Messiah; for certainly Messiah will be a Great Healer. Isa. 42:7 brings out the same thought. Turning to the life of the Lord Jesus Christ, what do we find? Much of his life was spent in healing the sick, curing the blind and benefitting the afflicted, as it was prophesied Messiah would do. Repeating again the words He Himself sent to the discouraged John in prison, "The blind receive their sight, the lame walk, the lepers are cleansed, the deaf hear, the dead are raised up, and the poor have the gospel preached to them." We see, at a glance that the Lord Jesus was willing to have His work compared with the work Messiah was to do, and adding no comment Himself, but let John, and the rest of the world judge Him and His work by the way it compared with what prophecy said would be the work of Messiah. Who could have acted more fairly? Such a wonderful Healer was Jesus that we read in Matt. 14:36, that they "besought him that they might only touch the hem of his garment: and as many as touched were made perfectly whole."

Jesus was ever ready to stand upon the merits of His own works, and be judged by them. As a further evidence that Jesus did what Messiah was to do, we have but to look at the many other cures which He did. Matt. 9, the healing of the two blind men; also a dumb demoniac; Mark 7, a deaf and dumb man healed; Luke 7, He heals the centurion's servant, and raises the son of the widow; John 5, gives sight to a man born blind; John 11, raises Lazareth from the dead, with numerous other miraculous healings during His wonderful life. Can it be expected that Messiah would or could do any more than Jesus did! Let us add one more testimony from Isa. 53:4, which says that "Surely he hath borne our griefs, and carried our sorrows: yet we did esteem him stricken, smitten of God, and afflicted." And we find same passage referred to in Matt. 8:17, thus: "That it might be fulfilled which was spoken by Esaias the prophet, saying, Himself took our infirmities, and bare our sicknesses."

Does not Jesus fulfill the prophecies about Messiah in this respect?

5. TO TRIUMPHANTLY ENTER THE JEWISH CAPITAL.

Says Zech. 9:9: "Rejoice greatly, O daughter of Zion; shout, O daughter of Jerusalem: behold, thy King cometh unto thee: he is just, and having salvation, lowly, and riding upon an ass, and upon a colt the foal of an ass."

Matthew 21:8, when giving a careful description of Jesus' last visit to Jerusalem, tells us that when He came near the city, He sent two of His disciples to get the colt, etc., and that He came into Jerusalem with a great throng following Him, and they cried out, "Hosanna to the Son of David: Blessed is he that cometh in the name of the Lord; Hosanna in the highest." Mark tells us the same story in 11:1–11, and Luke repeats it in 19:28–40, and adds that "Some of the Pharisees from among the multitude said unto him, Master, rebuke thy disciples. And He answered and said unto them, I tell you that, if these should hold their peace, the stones would immediately cry out." Matt. 21:4, 5, adds: "All this was done, that it might be fulfilled which was spoken by the prophet, saying, Tell ye the daughter of Sion, Behold, thy King cometh unto thee, meek, and sitting upon an ass, and a colt the foal of an ass."

Does not this triumphal entry of Jesus completely fulfill the prophecy of Zechariah about the coming of Messiah into Jerusalem? We leave the honest minded reader to give the verdict. As we draw closer to the consummation of Messiah's life, we find that the prophecies are both more numerous, as well as more explicit.

6. MESSIAH WILL BE REJECTED.

It is sad that humanity has fallen so low in sin that this point has to be inserted; but such is the fact, and it became a subject of prophecy many years before it was fulfilled. Of all the welcome visitors who could come into this sin-cursed world, certainly it would seem that Messiah, the One sent from God to deliver the people from their sins, would be the most welcome of all; yet away back in the history of the world, more than seven hundred years before the day for Him to appear, it was told by God, through His holy prophets, that when His redeemer should come to do the people good, to give them "new hearts," and to "write the law of God in their hearts," that, instead of welcoming Him with the greatest possible joy, the world would actually "reject" Him, and turn from Him in bitterness of heart and enmity towards Him! Oh! the depravity of a heart full of sin!!

Let us examine the passages, strange as it may sound, which refer to His rejection, and learn as well, how He was despitefully treated.

Isa. 53:3, says: "He is despised and rejected of men; a man of sorrows, and acquainted with grief: and we hid as it were our faces from him; he was despised, and we esteemed him not."

Does it seem possible that such a prophecy could ever have a fulfillment? That the very One, who coming to do us good, should receive such a reception from any people, and especially, from those whom He came to help? Does it seem possible that any people *could* be so sinful, and so forgetful of their own best interests, to say nothing of ingratitude, as to reject and *despise* the very best of all friends? The only business this great Messenger and Representative from the court of high heaven had in the world, was to "seek and to save the lost." Then can it be true that these very lost ones, for whom alone He came, can turn their backs upon Him, malign, maltreat, scourge, persecute, despise and murder Him, who came because He loved them so much? Oh! the miserable sinfulness of lost and depraved humanity! Shall we not blush with shame and trickling tears of repentance, when we examine and learn that He was so treated?

Have we not rejected Him in the past, or it may be that some reader is now rejecting Him in his heart. How can you do so? Let us examine and see how He was "despised" and "rejected" of men.

Isa. 49:7, says again: "Thus saith the Lord, the Redeemer of Israel, and his Holy One, to him whom man despiseth, to him whom the nation abhorreth." But a superficial examination of the facts show us that Jesus was "despised and rejected" of the men in His day, and in fact, He is "despised and rejected" of men, in this our day and age. When He was brought before Pilate, how was He treated? Matt. 27:22,23: "Pilate said unto them, What shall I do then with Jesus which is called Christ? They all say unto him, Let him be crucified. And the governor said, Why, what evil hath he done? But they cried out the more, saying, Let him be crucified." And so we find the same story from the pen of Mark 15:13,14: "And they cried out again, Crucify him. Then Pilate said unto them, Why, what evil hath he done? And they cried the more exceedingly, Crucify him."

Without quoting all that is said on this subject by each of the four gospel writers, we notice that Luke 23:18,23, and John 19:6,15, both tell the same story of the bitter hatred and rejection that Jesus received at the hands of the multitude.

Certainly no further evidence is needed to prove that Jesus was "despised and rejected" of men. John tells us in 1:11: "He came unto his own, and his own received him not." We can rest assured that he was "despised and rejected" of men, as the prophets said Messiah would be.

One thing let us do, in the study of this subject of Jesus being the Messiah of Jewish prophecy, that is, be honest enough with the subject and with ourselves to acknowledge that a point has been made when it is made, and never try, in the least, to evade the just conclusion.

CHAPTER VI.

ESSIAH'S ARREST AND DEATH.

WE now approach one of the most solemn parts of the Messiah's entire life; and very minute and plentiful are the prophecies now of the arrest and the death of the Messiah, and this is quite proper indeed; for if He had to bear the iniquity of the world; if He is to make atonement for our sins; if He is to be our substitute and Redeemer, how all-important it is for us to have definite data from which we may identify him, when he arrives in the world; and how particular we should be to know all the facts as to his death for us. While we thank God for the pure and unblemished life he lived, yet that pure life in and of itself *never* could have saved a single soul from perdition! I bless God with great gratitude in my heart, for the holy teachings that Jesus revealed to the world; but these holy teachings in and of themselves alone *never* could have saved a single sinner; it is also a matter of great gratitude that he was able to heal the sick, give eyes to the blind, raise the dead, and all the other miraculous deeds which he did; but these and all these above named could never raise a single sinner from the curse of the law. Up to this point we have not yet found anything in the life of either the Messiah, or the life of Jesus, that is able to save sinners; we must look further into the life or death for that which saves sinners. Had Jesus lived the life he did live, taught as he did teach, work wonders as he did work them, and yet had gone back to heaven from Bethany, and had not gone by Calvary, God could never have opened heaven's gates nor bid welcome to a single one of earth's lost sinners! O dear soul, remember that it was Calvary where Jesus did his work that saved sinners. O thou preacher of the gospel and worker for lost souls, if you omit Calvary from your sermons and work you have also left out salvation. Say as many pretty things about Jesus and his matchless life as your vocabulary may afford; paint him in all the fervent oratory and beauty that words are possibly capable of conveying; extol his wondrous life to the very limit to human exaltation; but in all this, if you leave Calvary out, you have but preached a christless Christ. Think of it, if you can, a crossless Christ! That is what preaching means which leaves out Calvary. Dear soul, you can not know what sin really is, till you come to Calvary; nor can you appreciate God's justice till you stand close by Calvary; nor can you know the "peace of God, which passeth understanding," till you have knelt low at Calvary. The gospel without Calvary is worthless; it is salt that has lost its savor, good for nothing. The road to heaven always leads right close by Calvary, and when you get out of that road, you are lost! Calvary's cross is the sinner's best friend, and none need ever hope for heaven who has not passed that way. It is said that "All roads lead to Rome." Yes, and all heavenly roads lead to Calvary. No wonder then, that God's prophets said so much about the death and sufferings of Messiah, when so much depends upon it. If the death of some one is to be the *only* hope you have for time and for eternity, how anxious you should be to know who that personage is, having the most definite particulars as to his identity, as well as what he will do for you.

God, seeing that just such a desire would be natural, has given us very accurate data from which to judge, and also to *know* the Messiah; and there are, therefore, more prophecies about his death than any other point in his entire life.

Jesus may have been ever so good a man, and he may fulfill every prophecy up to this point; but if he fails here, he has failed altogether; for this is the pivotal point around which all others revolve.

It is strange the way this point has been guarded and fortified, by the prophets of God. This truth of itself is sufficient to force conviction on any inquiring mind, that the hand of God *must have been* in it all; for the prophets of themselves would never have known that it is of so much importance to fortify so carefully this point in the life of Messiah, if they had been left to themselves; God told them what to write.

1. THE BETRAYAL.

The prophets are careful to tell us that Messiah should not be captured, but that he would be betrayed by a friend. They are careful to tell us the position of the one who should betray him.

(1.) THE BETRAYER.

The prophets foretold very distinctly that it would be no stranger who should betray Messiah into the hands of his enemies, but that it would be one very near him. Psa. 41:9: "Yea, mine own familiar friend in whom I trusted, which did eat my bread, hath lifted up his heel against me."

The betrayer of Messiah was to be one who was a friend, and not an enemy. Should it be an open enemy, or a stranger who betrays, it will fail to fulfill the prophecy. Let us see.

It would be superfluous to state here that Judas betrayed Him, as every child knows that; but we may ask the question, Who was Judas? and what relation did he sustain to the Lord Jesus? His position to the Savior is almost as well known, as it is known that he betrayed Him; for all know that he was the treasurer of the party that went with Jesus, as "He went about doing good," throughout all the lands of His earthly travels. This we learn from John 12:6 and 13:29. Externally a friend, though internally a thief, he had been with the company that went with Jesus, ever since a few days before the delivery of the great sermon on the mount, which was delivered during the very early ministry of the Lord Jesus in Galilee, as is recorded in both Mark 3:13–19, and Luke 6:12–16. Judas was among the very first of the disciples and was also an apostle, chosen with the rest of the twelve, and at the same time. See Matt. 10:1–4; Mark 3:13–19; Luke 6:13–16.

John 13:26,30, tells us that Jesus answered: "He it is, to whom I shall give a sop (or morsel), when I have dipped it. And when he had dipped the sop, he gave it to Judas Iscariot, the son of Simon. He then, having received the sop, went immediately out."

So also Matthew tells us the same story of the betrayal of Jesus by Judas, and that he did it with a sign of a kiss, as we read in Matt. 26:47f. So also John again speaks of him, 18:2,3.

Judas was the "familiar friend," who knew where Jesus was accustomed to go, and when He went. It was also he that was the "one that was trusted" with all the money of the entire party; and was also he that did "eat bread," as he received the sop from the hand of the Lord, as well as being one that was always with the Lord, and did eat of the bread that was the food of the party, and no doubt, ate many times of the food provided by the hands of the Lord, when the five thousand were fed, as well as the four thousand, and on numerous other occasions; eating with the Lord all the time, till he betrayed Him. Complete fulfillment is seen here.

(2.) THE PRICE PAID.

It may seem but a very small thing that the price which was to be paid for the delivering up of the Messiah should be a matter of prophecy, as well as the very *kind* of money to be used, and all this foretold centuries before the thing was to take place; but notice that both the amount and kind are foretold near seven hundred years before its fulfillment. Zechariah 11:12,13: "And I said unto them, If ye think good, give me my price; and if not, forbear. So they weighed for my price *thirty* pieces of silver. And the Lord said unto me, Cast it unto the potter: a goodly price that I was prized at of them. And I took the *thirty* pieces of silver, and cast them to the potter in the house of the Lord." We shall see how the treatment of Jesus corresponded with this strangely minute prophecy.

Matt. 26:15: "And said (Judas) unto them What will ye give me, and I will deliver him unto you? And they covenanted with him for *thirty* pieces of *silver.*"

(3.) WHAT WAS TO BE DONE WITH THE PRICE PAID.

It might seem even a smaller thing to tell what a dishonorable man would do with the money he had obtained by fraud; but it is not so much to follow up what he would do with it, as it is to show, *very minutely*, what was to be done, in every particular, concerning the *Great Messiah;* to point out all the minutia so clearly that you and I may know who this Great Messiah is. So we learn that prophecy tells us as carefully what shall be done with the price, as it tells us what the price is to be. Zech. 11:13, says that he was to "cast them to the potter *in the house of the Lord.*" Turn with me to Matthew 27:3-10, and learn what Judas *did* with the price paid him for Jesus. "Then Judas, which had betrayed him, when he saw that he was condemned, repented himself,* and brought

---

*The word here translated "Repented" is not the regular word used when referring to repentance and faith in the Lord Jesus. This word is the word in Greek, " Metamelomai," which means, "To have remorse," while the word used for repentance towards God, and is connected with faith, is " Metanoaoo," and a good short distinction of the two is that the first means simply "remorse," while the latter grieves for the intrinsic wrong itself.

the thirty pieces of silver to the chief priests and elders, saying, I have sinned in that I have betrayed innocent blood. And he *cast down the pieces of silver in the temple*, and went and hanged himself."

Let us notice four things that are very minutely and carefully stated: (a) The number of pieces, *thirty*. (b) The kind of money, *silver*. (c) What shall be done with it, "Buy the potter's field." (d) Where it should be appropriated to this purpose, "In the Lord's house, the temple." The passage quoted above, Matt. 27:3-10, tells us that all these things were done just as it was prophesied of Messiah, and all were done unto Jesus.

Dear candid reader, does not Jesus here completely fulfill the prophecy? Leaving it to your honesty, we pass to

(4.) THE SHEPHERD SMITTEN; THE SHEEP SCATTERED.

Zechariah again speaks to us, 13:7, and says concerning the effect of Jesus' being arrested: "Awake, O sword, against my Shepherd, and against the man that is my fellow, saith the Lord of hosts: smite the Shepherd, and the sheep shall be scattered."

Quite completely is this prophecy fulfilled in

Jesus, and he said it was so fulfilled, in Matt. 26:31: "Then saith Jesus unto them, All ye shall be offended because of me this night: for it is written, I will smite the Shepherd, and the sheep of the flock shall be scattered abroad." And Mark testifies to the same fact in 14:27. It is a fact that when Jesus was taken, the disciples were scattered. Is not Jesus the "smitten Shepherd," and His disciples the "scattered sheep?"

2. THE FALSE WITNESSES.

These false witnesses who would appear against the Messiah were not left unmentioned. David wrote concerning them more than a thousand years before they testified their falsehoods against the Messiah. Says David, Psa. 27:12: "Deliver me not over unto the will of mine enemies: for false witnesses are risen up against me, and such as breathe out cruelty."

So also the same writer mentioned this fact in Psa. 35:11, thus: "False witnesses did rise up; they laid to my charge things that I knew not." It would be superfluous to the Bible reader to say that such was the case with the Lord Jesus. We read this fact in Matt. 26:59–61, as follows: "Now the chief priests, and elders, and all the council, sought *false witnesses against Jesus*, to put him to death; But found none: yea, though *many false witnesses came*, yet found they none. At the last came *two false witnesses*, And said, This fellow said, I am able to destroy the temple of God, and to build it in three days." Jesus never made such a statement.

The complete fulfillment here is too striking not to be seen by the dullest mind, if not biased by prejudice. We humbly trust that there are none of that kind. Even if Jesus had said what they said He did, what was there in it to condemn a man to death?

3. TREATMENT AT THE CROSS.

We now come to a class of prophecies, which for care in statement, minuteness of description and vividness of the pictures, are equalled by nothing, except the completeness of fulfillment, which we find that the Lord Jesus did.

There are seventeen different and distinct prophecies as to the treatment of Messiah, when He comes to the cross. Let us be perfectly honest with these prophecies and with ourselves, and learn the truth, and all the truth, about them. Remember that they tell both what He himself will do, as well as what others will to do Him. It would be a comparatively easy thing to do, to fulfill partly the prophecies that Messiah was to do Himself; but how an impostor could succeed in getting His enemies to do the very things that are foretold they would do, we leave to the ingenuity of any one who is so foolish as to suppose that Jesus could have gotten them to do so. Let us examine the prophecies themselves.

(1.) WHAT MESSIAH HIMSELF WILL DO.

Prophecy tells us very clearly what Messiah will do, and for perspicuity, we arrange them in the following order:

a. HE WILL SUFFER FOR OTHERS.

Says Isa. 53:4: "Surely he hath borne our griefs, and carried our sorrows: yet we did esteem him stricken, smitten of God, and afflicted." So again in the same chapter, v. 5: "He was wounded for our transgressions; he was bruised for our iniquities: the chastisement of our peace was upon him; and with his stripes we are healed." So again the same thought in verse 12: "And he bare the sin of many." Certainly if these prophecies mean anything, they mean that Messiah should become the sin bearer for the people, would pay the penalty of our sins, or in short, would become our substitute, our "ransom" for the sins we have committed. Did Jesus suffer thus, is the question. I. Peter 3:18: "For Christ also hath once suffered for sins, the just for the unjust, that he might bring us to God." Also says the same writer, 2:21: "Because Christ also suffered for us." And v. 24: "Who his own self bare our sins in his own body on the tree." What can be plainer than that Jesus here is represented as having taken the place of the sinner, and that He bore the penalty that the sinner would have had to bear, had Christ not borne it for him? Then again, II. Cor. 5:21: "For he hath made him to be sin for us, who knew no sin." The very same thought is in the passage in I. Cor. 15:3: "For I delivered unto you first of all that which I also received, how that Christ died for our sins according to the Scriptures." Can words make it any plainer that Jesus died for the sins of the people? That was what Messiah was to do; and that is what Jesus did do. Does he not fulfill the prophecies?

b. HE WILL INTERCEDE FOR HIS PERSECUTORS.

In chapter IV., § 2, we noticed that he would be very patient under and during His afflictions; but here we can learn something more of His goodness and mercy during His trials; and we find what Jesus did is in perfect conformity to what Messiah was to do, in the following passages:

Psa. 109:4: "For my love they are my adversaries; but I give myself unto prayer." We find the same thought in Isa. 53:12: "He bare the sin of many, and made intercession for the transgressors." As to conformity of the actions of Jesus with this prophetic pattern, we have but to turn to Luke 23:34, and hear the words of Jesus Himself. Listen! "Father, forgive them; for they know not what they do." Paul makes the same point very strong, of Christ interceding for the sinner, in Rom. 8:34: "Who is he that condemneth? It is Christ that died, yea rather, that is risen again, who is even at the right hand of God, who also maketh intercession for us." So the writer of the Hebrews asserts the same, Heb. 7:25: "Wherefore he is able to save them to the uttermost, that come unto God by him, seeing that he ever liveth to make intercession for them." So again, we find the same doctrine in Heb. 9:24: "For Christ is not entered into the holy places made with hands, which are the figures of the true; but into heaven itself, now to appear in the presence of God for us." And to close this point of Christ being our intercessor and is praying for us, we quote I. John 2:1: "And if any man sin, we have an advocate with the Father, Jesus Christ the righteous."

If any one can read these passages referring to what Messiah will do, and then those that tell what Jesus *did* do, and fail to see that Jesus completely fulfills these Messianic prophecies, he must be a poor interpreter of Scripture.

c. MESSIAH WILL CRY UNTO GOD.

Psa. 22:1: "Eli, Eli, lama azavthani,"* "My God, my God, why hast thou forsaken me?" are the words of the prophet and psalmist David; giving utterance to the forsaken Son of

---
*The Hebrew reader will notice that the Savior did not quote the exact words of Psa. 22:1, in the Hebrew, as the word there used is "Azavthani," and the word the Savior used was "Sabachthani." The reason of this is very plain, when we notice a moment. The word "Azavthani" is good Hebrew, from "Azav," "To forsake," and when used with the accus. of the person, it signifies "To forsake one in great need;" but Jesus spoke in the Aramaic, and used the Aramaic word, "Sabachthani" having a very similar, if not an identical meaning. Mark 15:34, gives the whole sentence in Aramaic, "Eloi," etc.

God, as He hung helpless upon the cruel cross. Deserted of God, as the sinner who is not in Christ will be, if he turn not to Jesus. So we find it fulfilled in Jesus when Calvary's cross suspended Him, as told us by Matt. 27:46: "And about the ninth hour Jesus cried with a loud voice, saying, Eli, Eli, lama sabachthani?* that is to say, My God, my God, why hast thou forsaken me?"

The suffering of the cross and all the hoots and jeers of the rabble could be borne without a word of complaint; but when He had to endure the torture of being forsaken of the Father, as the unrepentant sinner will have to do, Jesus cried out, in the depth of His anguish, under the great crushing burden. It was more than He could bear in silence; it will be more than you can bear, O unrepentant soul, if you do not make thy peace with God through this sin-bearing Savior, when thou shalt be forsaken of the Righteous God of heaven! Oh! wilt thou not think and repent in time?

d. MESSIAH WILL DIE WITH MALEFACTORS.

We have the testimony of Isaiah on this point, 53:12: "And he was numbered with the transgressors." Three of the gospel writers

---
* See foot note, page 95.

join in telling that Jesus "was numbered with the transgressors." Matt. 27:38: "Then were there two thieves crucified with him; one on the right hand, and another on the left." To the same fact Mark gives his testimony, 15:27, 28: "And with him they crucify two thieves. And the Scripture was fulfilled, which saith, And he was numbered with the transgressors." Likewise says Luke 23:33: "And when they came to the place, which is called Calvary, there they crucified him, and the malefactors, one on the right hand, and the other on the left." Certainly there is no further testimony needed to establish the fact that Jesus was crucified with the transgressors, in the same way that the prophets said Messiah should be treated.

Let us accept facts when we have found them, and receive them even if they destroy the foundations of our dearest hopes and pet theories; for one truth is worth a thousand falsehoods, at any time; we therefore beg you, dear reader, for your own good, that you receive the truth at any cost of your own feelings or false hope you may have been hugging.

If Jesus did the things Messiah was to do, can it be otherwise than that He is that same

Messiah? May God's Holy Spirit help you to see that such is the real case.

(2.) WHAT OTHERS WILL DO UNTO MESSIAH.

We now begin a class of passages which tell us what others are to do to Messiah; and very minute and very explicit are they indeed.

a. WILL PIERCE HIS HANDS AND FEET.

The first passage we examine is one from David's writings, Psa. 22:16: "They pierce my hands and my feet." This passage is too plain to need any comment; we pass to another in which is mentioned much the same thought. Zech. 13:6: "And one shall say unto him, What are these wounds in thine hands?"

Let us turn to the words of John and see how all these things were fulfilled in Jesus; 20:25: "Except I shall see in his hands the print of the nails, and thrust my hand into his side, I will not believe." Thomas had seen the nails driven into those hands, and the spear thrust into His side, and he was slow to believe that the Master could be alive, after having suffered such cruelty; and he was anxious to see that he might know to a certainty that Jesus *was* alive again.

But hear Jesus when He met Thomas, v. 27, "Reach hither thy finger, and behold my hands; and reach hither thy hand, and thrust it into my side; and be not faithless, but believing."

Even doubting Thomas had seen enough to satisfy the most exacting mind as to the fact that Jesus was alive again; and he cried out, "My Lord and my God!"

There are yet so many Thomases in the world, still demanding that they shall see the Savior and thrust their hands into the wounds in His side and hands; the Savior has not suffered enough yet to satisfy the slow minds to believe, when the believing is for their benefit, and not for His good.

Further proof that the Savior had His hands and His feet pierced, certainly is not necessary; let us notice, in the next place, that

b. THEY WILL GIVE HIM VINEGAR TO DRINK.

Says Psa. 69:21: "They gave me also gall for my meat; and in my thirst they gave me vinegar to drink." He, who created all things, and by whom all things exist, when He wanted water, in His burning thirst, received naught but the biting vinegar! Thus does sinful humanity treat its loving God!

Matt. 27:34: "They gave him vinegar to drink mingled with gall: and when He had tasted thereof, He would not drink." Luke 23:36: "And the soldiers also mocked him, coming to him, and offering him vinegar." And so John also speaks the same, 19:29: "Now there was set a vessel full of vinegar: and they filled a sponge with vinegar, and put it upon hyssop, and put it to his mouth."

We have still more evidence that Jesus was treated as the prophets foretold they would treat the Messiah.

c. THEY WILL DIVIDE HIS GARMENTS; CAST LOTS FOR HIS COAT.

Does it seem a small thing to tell what will be done with the remaining clothing of a man that has been crucified with all the disgrace that a Roman government could attach to the crucifixion, and that the dying man could endure? But there is nothing too small for God to tell about His well-beloved Son, and here we find the words from the prophet a thousand years before it took place what would be done in this regard to the Messiah. See how minutely the prophet tells what shall be done!

Psa. 22:18: "They part my garments among them, and cast lots for my vesture." What was done with the clothes of Jesus? John 19:23,24: "Then the soldiers, when they had crucified Jesus, took his garments, made four parts, to every soldier a part; and also His coat: now the coat was without seam, ... Let us not rend it, but cast lots for it, whose shall it be: that the Scripture might be fulfilled, which saith, They parted my raiment among them, and for my vesture did they cast lots. These things therefore the soldiers did."

The soldiers were entirely ignorant of these prophecies; they were Roman soldiers and not acquainted with the Jewish prophecies. Yet the Omniscient God had spoken, saying that "these things" would occur. And now we see that the prophecy was completely fulfilled as He had said of His Son, that you and I may know Him, when He comes into the world. The next point is one that is quite peculiar indeed.

d. THEY WERE TO BREAK NO BONES, BUT PIERCE HIM.

This strange prophecy has a stranger sequel. Messiah was to be the true passover Lamb to which all the Old Testament lambs pointed: so in keeping with the law that no bone of a passover lamb should be broken; let us see what was done to Jesus.

Exodus 12:46: "Neither shall ye break a bone thereof" (i. e., of the passover lamb), and so, many other passages in the Old Testament. Then see the prophecy about Messiah. Psa. 34:20: "He keepeth all his bones: not one of them is broken." See how this was fulfilled in the case of Jesus. John 19:32-37: "Then came the soldiers, and brake the legs of the first, and of the other which was crucified with him: but when they came to Jesus, and saw that he was dead already, they brake not his legs." And says v. 36: "For these things were done, that the Scripture should be fulfilled, A bone of him shall not be broken." But notice again as to what followed. Zech. 12:10, says: "And they shall look upon me whom they have pierced." And we read in Rev. 1:7: "Behold, he cometh with clouds; and every eye shall see him, and they also which pierced him." Now turn to John 19:34 and 37: "But one of the soldiers with a spear pierced his side, and forthwith came there out blood and water." v. 37: "And again another Scripture saith, They shall look on him whom they pierced."

Wonderful is the complete fulfillment of prophecy here in the case of Jesus; how could anything be more perfectly fulfilled than Jesus fulfills this prophecy?

One says that he shall be pierced, and the others say that he shall have no bones broken. But the order of the Roman officer, Pilate, was exactly opposite to this prophecy. His order was to break the bones, and there was no order from him to the effect that he should be pierced. Pilate and God are in conflict with their prophecies and orders; and yet the prophecies of God are fulfilled to the letter, and the orders of Pilate, the Roman officer, was altogether disobeyed. They brake no bones, but they pierced him, as God's prophets said they would do. Strange fulfillment!!

c. THEY WILL DERIDE HIM.

Psa. 22:7,8: "All they that see me laugh me to scorn: they shoot out the lip, they shake the head, saying, He trusted on the Lord that he would deliver him: let him deliver him, seeing he delighted in him."

When Jesus hung upon the cross, notice how this was fulfilled. Matt. 27:39-44: "And they that passed by reviled him, wagging their heads, and saying, Thou that destroyest the temple, and buildest it in three days, save thyself. If thou be the Son of God, come down from the cross. Likewise also the chief priests, mocking him, with the scribes and elders, said, He saved others; himself he can not save. If he be the King of Israel, let him now come down from the cross, and we will believe him. He trusted in God; let him deliver him now, if he will have him: for he said, I am the Son of God."

Can you conceive of a more complete fulfillment of a prophecy than we find here, performed by his enemies? Their reviling and deriding was severe as it was prophesied, and done in the same way it was said it would be. Who can find an excuse to reject such clear testimony, and say he believes that Jesus was not the very one about whom this prophecy was spoken? We leave the doubter to answer.

f. THEY WILL BURY HIM WITH THE RICH.

We will close this chapter by calling attention to the fact that God's prophets said they would bury him with the rich. While we might mention still other points, but they are not quite so clear and positive as the others which we have examined, we will close with this one. We want to claim nothing that can not be fully established ; the last point is, then, they will bury him with the rich.

Notwithstanding the maltreatment he was to receive while He was alive, yet His body should have decent and respectful burial. Isaiah, the great Messianic prophet, tells us of this. Isa. 53:9: "And he made his grave with the wicked, and with the rich in his death." Matthew tells us of the fulfillment of this prophecy in the case of Jesus. Matt. 27:57–60: "When the even was come there came a rich man of Arimathea, named Joseph, who also himself was Jesus' disciple: He went to Pilate, and begged the body of Jesus. Then Pilate commanded the body to be delivered. And when Joseph had taken the body, he wrapped it in a clean linen cloth, and laid it in his own new tomb, which he had hewn out in the rock: and he rolled a great stone to the door of the sepulchre, and departed."

How an impostor could have had this done to his dead body, the very thing that prophecy said would be done to the body of the dead Messiah, we can not see, but will leave that to be answered by those who may doubt, if there can be any such.

The prophets had foretold, years and years

before Jesus came into the world, that Messiah would be treated in the way we have noticed in the last six points (from a to f), and we have seen that Jesus was treated in the identical manner which they had foretold; not only telling what Messiah Himself would do, but also what others would do unto Him; so that it is sheer folly to attempt to deny that they did fulfill, completely, the prophecies about Messiah.

CHAPTER VII.

MESSIAH TO RISE FROM THE DEAD.

WHILE the larger number of prophecies are found relating to the *death* of Messiah, yet we have additional prophecies as to His resurrection from the dead. His death on the cross being the crowning work for lost man, no wonder that there are so many things foretold concerning this one part of His wonderful life; but we have some few clear and pointed promises that He shall rise from the dead.

1. MESSIAH'S RESURRECTION.

We find David telling us of the resurrection of the Messiah, in Psa. 16:10: "For thou wilt not leave my soul in hell;* neither wilt thou suffer thine Holy One to see corruption." The numerous evidences that this was true with

---

*The word here translated "hell," is not the word for the place of torment, but is the word "Sheol," which means the "underworld," and is equivalent to the Greek word "hades," these two words mean the place of departed spirits, with no meaning of torment in them; so the expression means that God will not let Messiah stay in the grave.

Jesus, which are recorded in the New Testament, will not allow us to quote all of them; but a sufficient number to prove beyond the shadow of a doubt that it is true, let us proceed to notice.

Peter, being filled with the Holy Ghost, spoke, on the day of Pentecost, and the whole sermon was based upon the fact of the resurrection of the Lord Jesus. Acts 2:24–32, is full of this testimony. v. 24: "Whom God hath raised up, having loosed the pains of death;" and then he refers to the prophecy that is quoted above, and says that it applies here to the risen Lord. v. 27: "Because thou wilt not leave my soul in hell,* neither wilt thou suffer thine Holy One to see corruption." vs. 31,32: "He, seeing this before, spake of the resurrection of Christ, that his soul was not left in hell,* neither his flesh did see corruption. This Jesus hath God raised up, whereof we are witnesses." And also in Acts 4:10: "Be it known unto you all, ... that by the name of Jesus Christ of Nazareth, whom ye crucified, whom God raised from the dead," etc. Acts 3:15: "And killed the Prince of life, whom God hath raised from the dead, whereof we

---

*See foot note, page 107.

are witnesses." And also in Acts 10:40: "Him God raised up the third day, and shewed him openly." And then we omit *thirteen* more passages in Acts, and the Epistles, but notice a few in the Gospels. Matt. 28:6: "He is not here: for he is risen." Mark 16:6: "Be not affrighted: ye seek Jesus of Nazareth, which was crucified: he is not here; he is risen." Luke 24:6: "He is not here, but is risen." And John 20:11-16, tells the same story, and John 21:1, says: "After these things Jesus shewed himself again to the disciples at the sea of Tiberias." Certainly there is no more evidence needed to establish the fact that Jesus rose from the dead, as prophecy said Messiah would rise. From that Sunday morning in which He is said to have risen, the disciples never doubted that it was true; and the whole preaching of all the apostles and disciples was based entirely upon the fact that they had seen Him alive again, after He had been crucified; and they even went joyfully to their death rather than surrender the fact that Jesus had risen from the dead. They certainly knew what they asserted; for they were willing to give up life and everything, basing their hopes upon the fact that Jesus rose from the dead.

2. MESSIAH'S ASCENSION.

We read of the ascension of the Messiah in the Psalms, as we read of His resurrection. It was to be a great and joyous event, and the children were taught to sing of that day with great happiness and triumph, though they may not have understood as well then what they sang about, as we do now; but their prophets had foretold the wonderful event, and here is the prophecy. Psa. 68:18: "Thou hast ascended on high, thou hast led captivity captive: thou hast received gifts for men."

This strange and wonderful event must have sounded as a startling announcement, as they sang it, year after year, in their devotions; but the full meaning was to dawn upon the Israelites, bye and bye. Notice Mark's account of the event.

Mark 16:19: "So then, after the Lord had spoken unto them, he was received up into heaven." And says Luke also, 24:51: "And it came to pass, while he blessed them, he was parted from them, and carried up into heaven." And Luke says again, Acts 1:9: "And when he had spoken these things, while they beheld, he was taken up; and a cloud received him out of their sight." Paul states the same fact in I. Tim. 3:16; and it is referred to and trusted throughout the whole of the New Testament.

Is not Jesus the very One who was to rise from the dead, ascend up on high, and be the *Holy One of God?*

In the entire preaching of the apostles and the Christian church since the event occurred, this has been the theme for many sermons; the hope of all the discouraged; the point of certainty about which the preaching has always revolved; and the sermons and addresses found in the New Testament are meaningless jargon, if this fact be omitted. That Jesus rose from the dead; that he ascended up on high; that he is now, and has been since his ascension, with the Father, interceding for the sinner, are facts which are so fully brought out in the New Testament Scriptures that it is useless to discuss them at this point. A crucified, buried and risen Savior, who is the Redeemer of lost sinners, has been the theme of the orthodox Christians since the day Jesus ascended up on high.

This is the hope of the Christian, and has been, in all ages since that day. The encouragement to every worker; the inspiration to every missionary of the cross, wherever he may be, or has been, since Jesus went to heaven, the world over; and it is the life preserver that holds up the struggling souls on the stormy billows of this uneven life. Paul bases everything upon this one fact, I. Cor. 15:12–20; but he ends the argument with the 20th verse: "But now is Christ risen from the dead, and become the firstfruits of them that slept." And Jesus said himself, "Because I live, ye shall live also." The sum and substance of the whole Christian preaching might be reduced down to a very small compass, and that is, Jesus died for the lost sinner; was buried; and rose again on the third day, according to the Scriptures; that He ascended to heaven, and is now with the Father, interceding for the sinner. A crucified, risen, ascended Christ, is the full teachings of the New Testament.

CHAPTER VIII.

HIS KINGDOM TO SPREAD THE WORLD OVER.

ONE of the most interesting things about the Lord Jesus Christ's kingdom is that it is to be a

1. MISSIONARY KINGDOM.

This could not be understood by the Jews. They thought that God was all their own, and that no one else could have any of the benefits of the religion of their God. It seems to be the idea of very many of God's children to this day, that they are to enjoy the blessings of the religion of Jesus Christ, and let the rest of the world go without the Gospel and its blessings, just as the Jews wanted to do, in the days of the early work of the Apostles. Peter had to be driven into it, by the very force of circumstances, before he was at all willing to preach the Gospel to the company at the house of Cornelius, who was a Gentile. The other apostles were ready to excommunicate him because he went and preached the Word to the Gentiles; and he had to bring to bear a most unanswerable argument before they would hearken to his views; and this was, God had blessed the Gentiles in the very same way that He had blessed the Jews in the beginning; i. e., that God had given to the Gentiles the Holy Spirit as He had given Him to the Jews, and "who am I to withstand God?" The very same argument stands to-day as an unanswerable argument for mission work; God does convert the heathen now, as He converts those among Christian people; who should withstand God in not being a missionary? It was Paul that was trying to tell God what He ought to do, and that he (Paul) knew more about how to run the work than God did, Acts 22:17–22. But God said to him, "Depart: for I will send thee far hence unto the Gentiles." And the spirit of the people may easily be seen who were listening to Paul, for the account says, "And they gave him audience unto this word, and then lifted up their voices, and said, Away with such a fellow from the earth: for it is not fit that he should live."

Peter an anti-missionary; Paul an anti-missionary; the apostles anti-missionaries; the

the whole Jewish race anti-missionaries, till God had to sweep them off of their feet with evidence that it was His will the whole world should have the benefit of the blessed Gospel. And there are still men and women who claim to have enjoyed the blessings of the Gospel, who are yet "withstanding God" and refusing to send the Word to the dying millions, who have it not.

There can be no stronger evidence that God favors a movement than that He prospers it to the end it has been established; and when we see that God blesses the work, and converts men and women, through the labors of the missionaries, "who can withstand Him?"

Year after year brings the word of the hundreds and thousands who are converted in the heathen lands by the work of the missionaries; I ask, would God help a thing that is wrong? Yea, let Peter's question be asked with redoubled force, "*Who are you that you should withstand God?*"

But let us notice some of the prophecies that the kingdom of the Messiah should be a missionary kingdom. We notice the first from Psa. 72:8: "He shall have dominion also from sea to sea, and from the river unto the ends of the earth." And again from the pen of Zech. 9:10: "And his dominion shall be from sea even to sea, and from the river even to the ends of the earth." Some may claim that the prophecy of David referred to his own son, Solomon; but this can not be the limit of the prophecy; for it was never the case with the kingdom of Solomon, though he did have an extensive kingdom; but the prophecy can not refer to Solomon's kingdom, made by Zechariah, for Solomon had been dead well near *five hundred years* when Zechariah wrote his prophecy. Zechariah certainly referred to the Messiah's kingdom. David also says, Psa. 2:8: "Ask of me, and I shall give thee the heathen for thine inheritance, and the uttermost parts of the earth for thy possession."

The testimony of the gospel writers says that the kingdom of Jesus was to spread over the world. Luke 24:47: "And that repentance and remission of sins should be preached in his name among *all nations*, beginning at Jerusalem." This is too clear to need any comments. All nations were to have the benefit of the kingdom of Jesus, and were to enjoy the privileges of salvation, by having it offered to them, whether they accept it or not; this Christianity should be offered to all, by the God of grace. So again, we have the passage from Mark 16:15: "And He said unto them, Go ye into all the world, and preach the gospel to every creature." Oh! the expanse God's religion took, when Jesus had come and had made a gospel ready for the world's reception! Till then, it had been confined to the nation of the Jews; but now was the time for the Gentiles to receive benefit from the religion of Jesus Christ and the God of heaven. Oh! how the gates of heaven swung wide open when Jesus came!

2. WORK OF MISSIONS TO BE DONE BY HIS FOLLOWERS.

The prophecies of the Old Testament do not make it so plain who shall do the work of evangelizing the world, but it tells us clearly that all the nations shall have it.

Isa. 52:10: "All the ends of the earth shall see the salvation of our God." Here it is pointed that the gospel is to be taken to all the world, and that all shall have a chance to *see* the gospel and salvation of the Lord, whether they accept it or not. But the New Testament tells us plainly *who* is to carry on the work of taking the gospel to every creature in the world.

Says Jesus, Matt. 28:19: "Go ye (disciples) therefore (as he had all power given to him) and teach *all* nations, baptizing them in the name of the Father, and of the Son, and of the Holy Spirit." The disciples understood that Jesus wanted them to take the Gospel to every creature; for at once, as soon as they were scattered abroad from Jerusalem, Acts 8:4: "Therefore they that were scattered abroad, went *every where* preaching the Word."

Paul to the Gentiles, Peter to the Jews generally, Phillip to the eunuch of Ethiopia, Stephen to the people around him, and those that were "scattered abroad," went *every where*, telling the sweet story of the cross; and the kingdom was spread to the whole world. When the Phillippian church sent some aid to Paul, or as we would call it nowadays, had done some missionary work, Paul wrote them that he rejoiced much over their labor, and that he had "received of Epaphroditus the things which were sent from you, an odor of sweet smell, a sacrifice, well-pleasing to God." Phil. 4:18.

See how God was "well-pleased" with the missionary work that the Phillippian church had done; why will he not be pleased with the missionary work that any other church does *now?* But as we indicated in the previous section, we know that God is a missionary *now*; for he blesses the work that the missionaries are doing on the field, the same he blessed the work, when Paul and the other missionaries were at work; God, saving souls, sending the Holy Spirit in His office work. Following the missionary, day by day, blessing his labors, and bringing men and women to repentance and renewing their spirits, as He did in the days of the apostles. "Who are you, dear reader, to withstand God?" if you for a moment say that the work of missions shall not be carried on *now*, as the Lord has commanded us to do?

CHAPTER IX.

NEGATIVE VIEW OF THE LIFE OF JESUS.

SOME THINGS WHICH COULD NOT HAVE BEEN TRUE OF AN IMPOSTOR.

IT is sometimes heard from those who do not accept Jesus as the Messiah, that they will claim He was an impostor, and that He made claims to many things that were not His to claim. We present the following chapter for the very earnest consideration of all such persons.

When we begin to look at the unique position which Jesus occupied in the world, it will be seen as plainly as day that there are things which could not have been true if He had been an impostor. In the very nature of affairs, there are some, over which no man can have the least possible control, be he ever so wise, or careful, or good. We want to look at some of those things over which no man can have the very least control whatever.

1. No man can have the least possible control over the line of his ancestry, as to what line it shall be. Dear reader, you had no more control, nor no more to do with the particular *parentage* from whom you were born, than you had with the creation of the world; not a particle more. Now the Old Testament scriptures said Messiah was to be born of the line of *Abraham, Isaac, Jacob, Judah, Jesse,* and *David;* Jesus was born of this exact line, as we have learned.

2. No one can have aught to do as to *where* he is born. This event in the life of every one, has passed long before one is conscious of having birth at all; and there is as little possibility of one's having himself born here or there, as it is to become self-existent. This certainly is as clear as the point above named. But prophecy said that Messiah would be born in Bethlehem; Jesus was born in Bethlehem, as every one knows and as we have seen in the past pages.

3. A babe can have absolutely nothing to do with the *time when* he is to be born; but we see that the prophets said Messiah should be born *before* the descendants of Judah should cease to rule; Jesus was born at that time.

4. The same inability occurs as to who shall be the mother of a child, as it does as to who shall be in the line of ancestry. Yet we have seen that the prophets of God foretold that Messiah should be born of a *virgin*; it did not simply "happen" that Jesus was born of a *virgin* mother; it was indeed *the sign* chosen by God himself.

5. Very little indeed, could a babe have to do as to whether he should be persecuted or not, while a babe; but the prophets said Messiah would be persecuted; Jesus was so persecuted, as we have learned in our study.

6. A babe can have absolutely nothing to do with who comes to see him, while a babe; yet we learned that the Magi were to visit Messiah; they certainly did visit Jesus.

7. A babe can have nothing to do with being driven out of his native land, while yet an infant; but the prophets were very careful to tell us that Messiah would be driven out of his native land; Jesus was so driven out of his native land.

8. Neither can a babe have any thing to do with the nature he is to be born with; and yet we find that the prophecies tells us that Messiah should have a two-fold nature, human

and divine; Jesus certainly had this two-fold nature.

9. There is a point in the development of the kingdom of the Lord Jesus, with which he could have had but very little to do, had he been an impostor; and that is, to have another man, who up to this point in their lives were strangers, come and say certain things about him, if they had never met; but prophecy said that there would be a forerunner come before Messiah, who would prepare the way, and begin the work in the wilderness; Jesus did have just such a forerunner, and it appears that they had never met till the baptism of Jesus. See John 1:31.

10. No one can have just such a temper as they may choose: but prophecy said that Messiah would have a very gentle temper; Jesus did have such a temper, as the Bible so represents.

11. No one can simply choose to have just such a holiness as will be sure to please God; but the prophets said that when Messiah should come, he would have such a holiness, and the New Testament tells us that Jesus did have that very kind of holiness.

12. No man can so control other men that

they will reject him when he comes among them ; but the prophets said that when Messiah came, he would be rejected ; Jesus was rejected; as they said Messiah would be.

13. No man, not of God, could possibly do miracles such as are ascribed to Messiah ; but the prophets foretold that when Messiah came, he would do miracles, and very wonderful ones; Jesus did perform very wonderful miracles.

14. What control could any man have over the way he was to be betrayed? yet Scripture says that Messiah should be betrayed in a certain way; Jesus was betrayed in that very way.

15. What could any man have to do with the very amount and the very kind of money that should be given for his betrayal? yet the prophets told beforehand that Messiah would be betrayed for *thirty* pieces of *silver;* Jesus was betrayed for just that amount and that kind of money, *silver.*

16. Neither could any man have any thing to do with what should be done with the money paid for his betrayal; but prophecy said that the money given for the betrayal of Messiah would be given to the potter, and that it should be done in the house of the Lord ; and this was exactly what was done with the money that was given for the betrayal of Jesus.

17. What could any man do towards getting himself "smitten" and his disciples "scattered"? but the prophets said they would do this with Messiah; they did it precisely with Jesus.

18. A criminal can have naught to do with the kind of witnesses that are to be brought against him; but Scripture said that they would bring *false* witnesses against Messiah; they did bring *false* witnesses against Jesus.

19. When we come to the cross, there are few things that a false christ *might* have done; but there is the least possibility that he would do them. Yet there are many things which no one could have had done to himself. How could any one have his enemies pierce his hands and his feet? Yet we find that Scripture had foretold they would do this to the Messiah; they certainly did this to Jesus.

20. What could any one have had to do with their giving him vinegar to drink? But God's prophets said they would give Messiah vinegar to drink; and we know they gave vinegar to Jesus.

21. Could he have had any control as to what they should do with his garments? But Scripture had said long before, they would

"divide his garments among them and cast lots for his vesture." They certainly treated Jesus' garments in this way.

22. Could any criminal have aught to do with who should be crucified with him? Scripture said they would crucify Messiah with malefactors; we know that they crucified Jesus with such men.

23. Nor could he control at all as to where they should bury him. The prophets said they would bury Messiah with the rich; they so buried Jesus.

24. No criminal could control the people as to have them deride him; however, the Scriptures had spoken upon this point and said they would deride Messiah; they certainly derided Jesus.

25. Of course, an impostor could have no power at all to resurrect himself from the grave; yet the Scriptures say that Messiah would rise from the dead; Jesus rose.

26. No impostor could ascend up to heaven, but the prophets said Messiah would; Jesus did.

27. No impostor could carry on the work as the prophets said it would be carried on; but only lift up your eyes and behold the field, dear reader; is it possible that all these things

are true of the kingdom of Jesus and He not be Messiah? Oh! *Can it be?*

We close this chapter with a quotation from the valuable and readable book, "Many Infallible Proofs," by Rev. A. T. Pierson, D.D., and we commend the simple, tenable argument contained in the quotation. Taking one of the prophecies which Jesus made, he discusses the probability and non-probability of its being fulfilled. We quote, pp. 55, 56:

"To answer this proper doubt, consider the law of simple and compound probability. When a single prediction is made, about which there is but one feature, it may or it may not prove true; there is therefore one chance in two of its being fulfilled. For instance, suppose I say there is going to be a very hot summer—it may be hot or it may be mild—the chance of fulfillment is represented by the fraction one-half. This is the law of simple probability. If I introduce a second particular, I get into the region of compound probability. For instance, suppose I say, ... that June fifteenth will be very hot. Here are two predictions; one is that there will be extreme heat; the other, that that it will be on a certain day. Each prediction has a half chance of fulfillment; the compound probability is one-fourth, i. e., there is one chance in four that both predictions will be verified. Every new feature added makes the fraction of probability smaller.

"In this prophecy, there is no vague general prediction; but a startling array of minute particulars. Our Lord draws the portrait of the coming event in detail; time, place, persons, marked circumstances, all introducing peculiar features which leave no doubt as to our power to recognize the event, if it shall look like its portrait. We find some twenty-five distinct predictions here, and, on the law of compound probability, the chance of their all meeting in one event, is as *one in nearly twenty millions*, i. e., the fraction that represents the chance of probability is one-half raised to its twenty-fourth power, or about one twenty-millionth chance!"

With these simple rules of probability before us, and every fair-minded reader can see that they are perfectly reliable, let us notice how many chances there are that the events in the life of Jesus of Nazareth could have so completely fulfilled all the twenty-seven points, which we have noticed above they did. The fraction here in His case would have to be raised to the twenty-sixth power, or two powers higher than Dr. Pierson has computed, or multiplying the *twenty millions* by two twice more, and it would be *one chance in eighty millions.*

Enormous as this denominator is, and with but this one chance in eighty millions that He could have been an impostor, yet the fraction is not, *by any means,* raised to the proper denominator; for each one of these twenty-seven points of prophecy has numerous particulars connected and included in it; so that we must count up all the different features of particularity which are to be found in each one of these twenty-seven points; and then raise the fraction of one-half to the power represented by all these particulars combined. There are not less than *ten* particulars, on the general average, of each of these twenty-seven points mentioned above, making two hundred and seventy particulars, all of which must be met in order that Jesus the Nazarene shall fulfill all the Messianic prophecies, and which we have learned that He did fulfill. Now according to the law of probability, which we have just learned, the fraction one-half must be multiplied by itself two hundred and sixty-nine times; and that will represent the *one* chance which He had in the millions represented by the denominator, that Jesus *could have* done what He did, and still be an impostor! Such an enormous denominator as this will produce, is simply beyond all comprehension; it takes *sixty places* of figures to represent it, over five hundred and forty-four *octo-decillions!!* A number clear out of all our experiences to calculate or comprehend!!!

Now upon the common, plain law of probability, there is but *one* chance in these five hundred and forty-four octo-decillions for Jesus to have been an impostor, and then do all the things that He did do. Who is the credulous one, the man who accepts all this enormous proof that Jesus was the Messiah, and receives and follows Him as such? Or the man who will cling to this *one chance* in these trillions times trillions?

Oh! the "many infallible proofs" that Jesus is the Messiah!!

Here is how the fraction would stand in real figures:

$$\frac{1}{544{,}567{,}902{,}154{,}708{,}736{,}674{,}183{,}077{,}786{,}497{,}976{,}000{,}000{,}000{,}000{,}000{,}000{,}000{,}000}$$

CHAPTER X.

SOME UNAVOIDABLE CONCLUSIONS.

DEAR reader, the object of the preceding book has been to prove one thing, one central thought that has pervaded all these chapters; it has been the reason for the writing of this book, and we wish to impress that thought upon you before we bid you adieu; and that thought is, the one often repeated, *Jesus is the Messiah of Prophecy*, and if the Messiah, then there are some things else that must be true. May the Holy Spirit of God aid you to see them.

1. If Jesus is the Christ, Messiah (for both mean the same thing), then He is God's own chosen Mediator to this world to save sinners.

God had been preparing the world for years for His coming, and has told and foretold, time and again, that He was coming to save sinners. Hundreds of years was God preparing the world for the coming of this Savior of sinners.

2. Then Jesus is the way, the *only* way.

God has not a number of ways of saving sinners, but *only one way*. He does not save me one way, you another, and your neighbor by still another way, and so on, giving each of us our choice as to how we shall be saved; but He saves sinners by *only one way*. And that way is *only* by Jesus Christ. See what the Scripture says, I. Tim. 2:5: "For there is one God, and *one mediator* between God and men, the man Christ Jesus." Do you not see the utter uselessness of trying to be reconciled to God *only* by the way He has ordained, through Jesus Christ?

Jesus is *the only way*, as stated by another Scripture, Acts 4:12: "Neither is there salvation in any other: for there is none other name under heaven given among men, whereby we *must* be saved." O, dear soul, there is absolutely no hope for you out of this Jesus as your personal Savior.

3. Won't you be reconciled to God by Jesus?

Will you not take him as your own personal Savior *now?* Delays are very dangerous; sin grows stronger and your power to resist grows weaker; time flies away so fast, bringing you nearer and nearer to eternity, and eternity is so long, and you are so poorly prepared; yea, if you be out of Christ, you are not prepared at all to enter eternity. May the Holy Spirit lead you to accept this blessed Savior as your Savior. May God so bless you!

PART II.

THE PROPHECIES FULFILLED.

PROPHECIES AND THEIR FULFILLMENTS IN PARALLEL COLUMNS.

CHAPTER I.

THE COMING MESSIAH.

1. GENERAL PROMISES OF HIS COMING.

Num. 24:17:

"I shall see him, but not now: I shall behold him, but not nigh: there shall come a Star out of Jacob, and a Sceptre shall rise out of Israel, and shall smite the corners of Moab."

Isa. 59:20:

"And the Redeemer shall come to Zion, and unto them that turn from transgression in Jacob, saith the Lord."

FULFILLED IN JESUS.

Luke 2:1,7:

"And it came to pass in those days, that there went out a decree from Cesar Augustus, that all the world should be taxed. And she brought forth her first born son, and wrapped him in swaddling clothes, and laid him in a manger."

(This was just before Herod died, the last ruler of the tribe of Judah, [though Archaelaus, a son

Haggai 2:7:
"And I will shake all nations, and the Desire of all nations shall come: and I will fill this house with glory, saith the Lord of hosts."

2. WHEN MESSIAH SHOULD COME.

Gen. 49:10:
"The sceptre shall not depart from Judah, nor a lawgiver from between his feet, until *Shiloh* come: and unto him shall the gathering of the people be."

Dan. 9:24,25:
"Seventy weeks are determined upon thy people and upon thy holy city, to finish the transgression, and to make an end of sins, and to make reconciliation for iniquity, and to bring in everlasting righteousness, and to seal up the vision and prophecy and to anoint the Most Holy. Know therefore and understand, that from the going forth

of this Herod, did rule for a short time after,] Herod was not a Jew, but his wife was a daughter of Hyrcanus, and her name was Mariamne. Herod died in the year A. D. 4, when Jesus was about eight years old.)

WHEN JESUS CAME.

(This commandment to rebuild the temple was made by Artaxerxes Longimanus, B. C. 457, as we can learn from the seventh chapter of Ezra. The "seventy weeks" here mentioned are to be interpreted according to the way the Bible interprets itself elsewhere; for instance, Num. 14:34, it says: "Each day for a year;" and again in Ezek. 4:6: "I have appointed thee each day for a year;" and with this understanding of this passage, it means a week of years; so that the seventy weeks mean four hundred and ninety years; if this number be added to the year B. C. 457, it of the commandment to restore and to build Jerusalem, unto the Messiah, the Prince, shall be seven weeks, and threescore and two weeks."

Dan. 2:44:
"And in the days of these kings shall the God of heaven set up a kingdom, which shall never be destroyed: and the kingdom shall not be left to other people, but it shall break in pieces and consume all these kingdoms, and it shall stand forever."

brings us to the year A.D. 33, the time when Jesus was crucified.)

3. THE PLACE OF HIS BIRTH.

(1.) THE TOWN NAMED.

Micah 5:2:
"But thou, Beth-lehem Ephratah, though thou be little among the thousands of Judah, yet out of thee shall *He* come forth unto me that is to be *Ruler* in Israel; whose goings forth have been from of old, from everlasting."

PLACE OF THE BIRTH OF JESUS.

BORN IN SAME TOWN.

Matt. 2:1-6:
"Now when Jesus was born in Bethlehem of Judea in the days of Herod the king, behold, there came wise men from the east to Jerusalem. When Herod the king had heard these things, he was troubled, and all Jerusalem with him. And when he had gathered all the chief priests and the scribes of

(2.) THE TOWN GENERALLY KNOWN.

(See how readily the chief priests and scribes *knew* where Messiah was to be born.)

the people together, he demanded of them where Christ should be born. And they said unto him, In Bethlehem of Judea: for thus it is written by the prophet, And thou Bethlehem, in the land of Juda, art not the least among the princes of Juda: for out of thee shall come a Governor, that shall rule my people Israel."

Luke 2:4,5,7:

"And Joseph also went up from Galilee, out of the city of Nazareth, into Judea, unto the city of David, which is called Bethlehem, (because he was of the house and lineage of David,) To be taxed with Mary his espoused wife, And she brought forth her first-born son, and wrapped him in swaddling clothes, and laid him in a manger."

4. MANNER OF MESSIAH'S BIRTH.

(1.) MESSIAH'S "SIGN."

Isa. 7:14:

"Therefore the Lord

MANNER OF JESUS' BIRTH.

JESUS' "SIGN."

Luke 1:26,27,31,32:

"Gabriel was sent from

himself shall give you a sign; Behold, a *virgin shall conceive*, and bear a son, and shall call his name *Immanuel.*"

(2.) MESSIAH'S NAMES.
Isa. 9:6:
"For unto us a child is born, unto us a son is given: and the government shall be upon his shoulder: and his name shall be called Wonderful Counsellor, The mighty God, The everlasting Father, The Prince of Peace."

God .... To a *virgin* .... and the virgin's name was Mary; And the angel said unto her, Fear not Mary: for thou hast found favour with God. And, behold, thou shalt conceive in thy womb, and bring forth a son, and shalt call his name JESUS. He shall be great, and shall be called the Son of the Highest; and the Lord God shall give unto him the throne of his Father David: And he shall reign over the house of Jacob for ever; and of his kingdom there shall be no end."

Luke 2:11:
"For unto you is born this day in the city of David a Savior, which is Christ the Lord. And this shall be a sign unto you: Ye shall find the babe wrapped in swaddling clothes, lying in a manger."

CHAPTER II.

MESSIAH'S RECEPTION IN THE WORLD.

1. THE MAGI TO WORSHIP.

Psa. 72:10,15:

"The kings of Tarshish and of the isles shall bring presents: the kings of Sheba and Seba shall offer gifts. And he shall live, and to him shall be given of the gold of Sheba: prayer also shall be made for him continually; and daily shall he be praised."

THEY DID WORSHIP JESUS.

Matt. 2:1,2:

"Now when Jesus was born in Bethlehem of Judea in the days of Herod the king, behold, there came wise men from the east to Jerusalem, Saying, Where is he that is born King of the Jews? for we have seen his star in the east, and are come to worship him."

2. PERSECUTED AT BIRTH.

Jer. 31:15:

"Thus saith the Lord: A voice was heard in Ramah, lamentation and bitter weeping; Rahel weeping for her children refused to be comforted for her children, because they were not."

JESUS WAS PERSECUTED.

Matt. 2:16-18:

"Then Herod, when he saw that he was mocked of the wise men, was exceeding wroth, and sent forth, and slew all the children that were in Bethlehem, and in all the coasts thereof, from two years old and under, according to the time which he had diligently inquired of the wise men. Then was fulfilled that which was spoken by Jeremy the prophet, saying: In Rama was there a voice heard, lamentation, and weeping, and great mourning, Rachel weeping for her children, and would not be comforted, because they are not."

3. MESSIAH TO BE DRIVEN FROM HIS COUNTRY.

Hosea 11:1:
"And called my son out of Egypt."

JESUS WAS DRIVEN FROM HIS COUNTRY.

Matt. 2:14,15:
"When he arose, he took the young child and his mother by night, and departed into Egypt: And was there until the death of Herod: that it might be fulfilled which was spoken of the Lord by the prophet, saying, Out of Egypt have I called my son."

CHAPTER III.

NATURES OF THE COMING MESSIAH.

1. HUMAN NATURE: HIS ANCESTRY.

(1.) TO BE OF THE SEED OF ABRAHAM.

Gen. 12:3:
"And in thee (Abraham) shall all families of the earth be blessed."

Gen. 22:18:
"And in thy (Abraham) seed shall all the nations of the earth be blessed; because thou hast obeyed my voice."

(The same thought may be found in Gen. 18:18; 26:4, and 28:14.)

(2.) AND OF THE SEED OF ISAAC.

Gen. 21:12:
"For in Isaac shall thy seed be called."

ANCESTRY OF JESUS.

Matt. 1:1-16:
"The book of the generation of Jesus Christ, the son of David, the son of Abraham. *Abraham* begat *Isaac;* and Isaac begat *Jacob;* and Jacob begat *Judas* and his brethren; and Judas begat Phares and Zara of Thamar; and Phares begat Esrom; and Esrom begat Aram; And Aram begat Aminadab; and Aminadab begat Naasson; and Naasson begat Salmon; and Salmon begat Booz of Rachab; and Booz begat Obed of Ruth; and Obed begat *Jesse;* and Jesse begat *David* the king," etc.

NATURES OF THE COMING MESSIAH. 143

(3.) AND THE SEED OF JACOB.

Num. 24:17,19:
"I shall see him, but not now: I shall behold him, but not nigh: there shall come a Star out of Jacob, and a Sceptre shall rise out of Israel. Out of Jacob shall come he that shall have dominion."

(4.) AND OF THE SEED OF JUDAH.

Gen. 49:10:
"The sceptre shall not depart from Judah, nor a lawgiver from between his feet, until *Shiloh* come; and unto him shall the gathering of the people be."

Deut. 18:15,18:
"The Lord thy God will raise up unto thee a Prophet from the midst of thee, of thy brethren, like unto me; unto him ye shall hearken. I will raise them up a Prophet from among their brethren, like unto thee, and will put my words in his mouth; and he shall speak unto them

Luke 3:31-34:
"Nathan, which was the son of *David*, which was the son of Jesse, which was the son of Obed, which was the son of Booz, which was the son of Salmon, which was the son of Naasson, which was the son of Aminadab, which was the son of Aram, which was the son of Esrom, which was the son of Phares, which was the son of Juda, which was the son of *Jacob*, which was the son of *Isaac*, which was the son of *Abraham*, which was the son of Thara," etc.

all that I shall command him."

(5.) AND OF THE SEED OF JESSE.

Isa. 11:1,10:
"And there shall come forth a rod out of the stem of Jesse, and a Branch shall grow out of his roots: And in that day there shall be a root of Jesse which shall stand for an ensign of the people; to it shall the Gentiles seek."

John 1:45:
"Philip findeth Nathanael and said unto him, We have found him of whom Moses in the law, and the prophets, did write, Jesus of Nazareth, the son of Joseph."

(6.) AND OF DAVID.

Psa. 89:3,4:
"I have made a covenant with my chosen, I have sworn unto David my servant, Thy seed will I establish for ever, and build up thy throne to all generations." Also verses 29 and 36.

Jer. 23:5,6:
"Behold, the days come, saith the Lord, that I will raise unto David a righteous Branch, and a King shall reign and prosper, and shall execute judgment and justice in the

earth. In his days Judah shall be saved, and Israel shall dwell safely: and this is his name, THE LORD, OUR RIGHTEOUSNESS."

2. DIVINE NATURE OF MESSIAH.

Isa. 25:9:
"And it shall be said in that day, Lo, this is our God: we have waited for him, and he will save us: this is the Lord; we have waited for him, we will be glad and rejoice in his salvation."

Isa. 9:6:
"For unto us a child is born, unto us a Son is given: and the government shall be upon his shoulder; and his name shall be called Wonderful Counsellor, Mighty God, The Everlasting Father, The Prince of Peace."

DIVINITY OF JESUS.

John 1:1-5:
"In the beginning was the Word, and the Word was with God, and the Word was God. The same was in the beginning with God. All things were made by him; and without him was not any thing made that was made. In him was life; and the life was the light of men. And the light shineth in the darkness; and the darkness comprehended it not."

I. Cor. 1:30:
"But of him are ye in Christ Jesus, who of God is made unto us wisdom, and righteousness, and sanctification, and redemption."

Phil. 2:6:
"Who, being in the form of God, thought it

not robbery to be equal with God."

John 5:18:

"Therefore the Jews sought the more to kill him, because he had not only broken the sabbath, but said also that God was his Father, making himself equal with God."

CHAPTER IV.

MESSIAH AND HIS DOCTRINES.

1. MESSIAH'S GENTLE-
NESS.
(1.) AS A TENDER SHEP-
HERD.
Isa. 40:11:
"He shall feed his flock like a shepherd: he shall gather the lambs with his arm, and carry them in his bosom."
Ezek. 34:23:
"And I will set up *one* Shepherd over them, and he shall feed them, my servant (see foot note, Part I. in loco): he shall feed them, and he shall be their shepherd."
Psa. 23:1:
"The Lord is my shepherd; I shall not want."

GENTLENESS OF JESUS.

John 10:11:
"I am the good Shepherd: the good Shepherd giveth his life for the sheep."
Heb. 13:20:
"Now the God of peace, that brought again from the dead our Lord Jesus, that great Shepherd of the sheep, through the blood of the everlasting covenant."
I. Peter 2:25:
"For ye were as sheep going astray; but are now returned unto the Shepherd and Bishop of your souls."
I. Peter 5:4:
"And when the chief Shepherd shall appear, ye

shall receive a crown of glory."

(2.) A MAN OF MEEKNESS.

Isa. 42:2,3:

"He shall not cry, nor lift up, nor cause his voice to be heard in the street. A bruised reed shall he not break, and the smoking flax shall he not quench."

Zech. 9:9:

"Behold, thy King cometh unto thee: He is just, and having salvation; lowly, and riding upon an ass."

JESUS WAS VERY MEEK.

Matt. 12:19,20:

"He shall not strive, nor cry; neither shall any man hear his voice in the streets. A bruised reed shall he not break, and smoking flax shall he not quench."

Matt. 21:4,5:

"All this was done, that it might be fulfilled which was spoken by the prophet, saying, Tell ye the daughter of Sion, Behold, thy King cometh unto thee, meek, and sitting upon an ass."

(3.) WELL PLEASING TO GOD.

Isa. 42:1:

"Behold my servant, whom I uphold; mine elect, in whom my soul delighteth; I have put my Spirit upon him: he shall bring forth judgment to the Gentiles."

JESUS WAS WELL PLEASING.

Matt. 3:17:

"This is my beloved Son, in whom I am well pleased."

Matt. 12:17,18:

"That it might be fulfilled which was spoken by Esaias the prophet, saying, Behold my servant, whom I have chosen;

my beloved, in whom my soul is well pleased."
Matt. 17:5:
"This is my beloved Son, in whom I am well pleased; hear ye him."

2. PATIENT UNDER SUFFERING.

(1.) WILL BE SORELY MALTREATED.

Isa. 50:6:
"I gave my back to the smiters, and my cheek to them that plucked off the hair: I hid not my face from shame and spitting."
Lam. 3:30:
"He giveth his cheek to him that smiteth him: he is filled full with reproach."

JESUS WAS PATIENT.

(1.) HE WAS SORELY MALTREATED.

Matt. 26:67,68:
"Then did they spit in his face, and buffeted him; and others smote him with the palms of their hands, saying, Prophesy unto us, thou Christ, Who is he that smote thee?"
Matt. 27:30:
"And they spit upon him, and took the reed, and smote him on the head."
Mark 14:65:
"And some began to spit on him, and to cover his face, and to buffet him, and to say unto him, Prophesy: and the servants did strike him with the palms of their hands."
Luke 22:63-65:
"And the men that held Jesus mocked him, and

smote him. And when they had blindfolded him, they struck him on the face, and asked him, saying, Prophesy, who is it that smote thee? And many other things blasphemously spake they against him."

Matt. 27:26:

"And when he had scourged Jesus, he delivered him to be crucified."

Mark 15:15:

"And so Pilate, willing to content the people, released Barabbas unto them, and delivered Jesus, when he had scourged him, to be crucified."

John 19:1:

"Then Pilate therefore took Jesus, and scourged him."

(2.) MESSIAH WILL BE SILENT WHEN AFFLICTED.

Isa. 53:7:

"He was oppressed, and he was afflicted, yet he opened not his mouth: he is brought as a lamb to the slaughter, and as a sheep before her shearers

JESUS WAS SILENT.

Matt. 26:62,63:

"And the high priest arose, and said unto him, Answerest thou nothing? what is it which these witness against thee? But Jesus held his peace."

is dumb, so he openeth not his mouth."

Psa. 109:4:
"For my love they are my adversaries: but I give myself unto prayer."

Matt. 27:12-14:
"And when he was accused of the chief priests and elders, he answered nothing. Then said Pilate unto him, hearest thou not how many things they witness against thee? And he answered him to never a word; insomuch that the governor marvelled greatly."

3. MESSIAH'S DOCTRINES.

(1.) HIS SCEPTRE ONE OF RIGHTEOUSNESS AND LOVE.

Psa. 45:6,7:
"Thy throne, O God, is for ever and ever: the sceptre of thy kingdom is a right sceptre. Thou lovest righteousness, and hatest wickedness: therefore God, thy God, hath anointed thee with the oil of gladness above thy fellows."

JESUS' DOCTRINES.

Heb. 1:8,9:
"But unto the Son he saith, Thy throne, O God, is for ever and ever: a sceptre of righteousness is the sceptre of thy kingdom. Thou hast loved righteousness, and hated iniquity; therefore God, even thy God, hath anointed thee with the oil of gladness above thy fellows."

John 13:34:
"A new commandment I give unto you, That ye love one another; as I

have loved you, that ye also love one another."

John 15:12:

"This is my commandment, That ye love one another, as I have loved you."

John 15:17:

"These things I command you, that ye love one another."

I. Thess. 4:9:

"But as touching brotherly love ye need not that I write unto you: for ye yourselves are taught of God, to love one another."

Matt. 22:39:

"And the second is like unto it, Thou shalt love thy neighbor as thyself."

(2.) REGENERATION PROMISED.

Jer. 31:33:

"But this shall be the covenant that I will make with the house of Israel: After those days, saith the Lord, I will put my law in their inward parts, and write it in their hearts; and will be their God, and they shall be my people."

(1.) JESUS TAUGHT REGENERATION.

John 3:3,7:

"Jesus answered and said unto him, Verily, verily, I say unto thee, Except a man be born again, he cannot see the kingdom of God. Marvel not that I said unto thee, Ye must be born again."

II. Cor. 5:17:

"If any man be in

Jer. 32:39:
"And I will give them one heart, and one way, that they may fear for ever."

Ezek. 36:26:
"A new heart also will I give you."

(3.) THE HOLY SPIRIT PROMISED.

Ezek. 11:19:
"I will put a new spirit within you; and I will take away the stony heart out of their flesh."

Ezek. 36:26,27:
"And a new spirit will I put within you: And I will put my Spirit within you, and cause you to walk in my statutes, and ye shall keep my judgments, and do them."

Christ, he is a new creature: old things are passed away; behold, all things are become new."

HOLY SPIRIT SENT BY JESUS.

John 16:7:
"It is expedient for you that I go away: for if I go not away, the Comforter will not come unto you; but if I depart, I will send him unto you."

John 15:26:
"But when the Comforter is come, whom I will send unto you from the Father."

THE SPIRIT SENT.

Acts 2:1,4:
"And when the day of Pentecost was fully come, ... They were all filled with the Holy Ghost, and began to speak with other tongues, as the Spirit gave them utterance."

CHAPTER V.

MESSIAH'S LIFE AND LABORS.

1. THE BEGINNING OF HIS KINGDOM.

(1.) THE FORERUNNER.

Mal. 4:5:
"Behold, I will send you Elijah the prophet before the coming of the great and dreadful day of the Lord."

Josephus Antiq., b. 18, ch. 5, § 2, says:
"Now some of the Jews thought that the destruction of Herod's army (in the battle with Aretas, king of Arabia) came from God; and that very justly as a punishment of what he did against John who is called 'The Baptist.' For Herod slew him, who was a good man, and commanded the Jews to exercise virtue; both as to righteousness toward one another, and piety to-

Mark 1:1-3:
"The beginning of the Gospel of Jesus Christ, the Son of God: As it is written in the prophets, Behold, I send my messenger before thy face, which shall prepare thy way before thee. The voice of one crying in the wilderness, Prepare ye the way of the Lord, make his paths straight."

Luke 3:3,4:
"And he came into all the country about Jordan, preaching the baptism of repentance for the remission of sins; As it is written in the book of the words of Esaias the prophet, saying, The voice of one crying in the

wards God, and so to come to baptism, for that the washing with water would be acceptable to Him, if they made use of it, not in order to putting away or the remission of some sins only: supposing still the soul was thoroughly purified beforehand by righteousness.

Now, when many others came in crowds around him, ... Herod .... thought it best by putting him to death, to prevent mischief he might cause. Accordingly he was sent to prison out of Herod's suspicious temper, to Machaerus, the castle I before mentioned, and was there put to death."

wilderness, Prepare ye the way of the Lord, make his paths straight."

John 1:19-23:

"And this is the record of John, when the Jews sent priests and Levites from Jerusalem to ask him, Who art thou? And he confessed, and denied not; but confessed, I am not the Christ. And they asked him, What then? Art thou Elias? And he saith, I am not. Art thou that prophet? and he answered, No. Then said they unto him, Who art thou? that we may give an answer to them that sent us. What sayest thou of thyself? He said, I am the voice of one crying in the wilderness, Make straight the way of the Lord, as said the prophet Esaias."

Matt. 17:12,13:

"But I say unto you, That Elias is come already, and they knew him not, but have done unto him whatsoever they listed. Likewise shall also the Son of man suffer of them. Then the disciples understood that he spake unto them of John the Baptist."

(2.) THE WILDERNESS CRY.

Isa. 40:3:
"The voice of him that crieth in the wilderness, Prepare ye the way of the Lord, make straight in the desert a highway for our God."

Matt. 3:1-3:
"In those days came John the Baptist, preaching in the wilderness of Judea, and saying, Repent ye: for the kingdom of heaven is at hand. For this is he that was spoken of by the prophet Esaias, saying, The voice of one crying in the wilderness, Prepare ye the way of the Lord, make his paths straight."

(3.) THE WAY PREPARED.

Mal. 3:1:
"Behold, I will send my messenger, and he shall prepare the way before me: and the Lord whom ye seek, shall suddenly come to his temple, even the messenger of the covenant, whom ye delight in: behold, he shall come, saith the Lord of hosts."

Matt. 11:9,10:
"But what went ye out to see? A prophet? yea, I say unto you, and more than a prophet. For this is he, of whom it is written, Behold, I send my messenger before thy face, which shall prepare thy way before thee. Verily I say unto you, Among them that are born of women there hath not

risen a greater than John the Baptist."

Luke 1:76:

"And thou, child, shalt be called the prophet of the Highest: for thou shalt go before the face of the Lord to prepare his ways. To give knowledge of salvation unto his people by the remission of their sins."

Luke 1:17:

"And he shall go before him in the spirit and power of Elias, to turn the hearts of the fathers to the children, and the disobedient to the wisdom of the just; to make ready a people prepared for the Lord."

Matt. 11:14:

"And if ye will receive it, this is Elias, which was for to come."

Mark 9:13:

"But I say unto you, That Elias is indeed come, and they have done unto him whatsoever they listed, as it is written of him."

2. Messiah to be a Preacher of the Gospel.

Isa. 61:1–3:

"The Spirit of the Lord God is upon me; because the Lord hath anointed me to preach good tidings unto the meek; he hath sent me to bind up the broken hearted, to proclaim liberty to the captives, and the opening of the prison to them that are bound: To proclaim the acceptable year of the Lord, and the day of vengeance of our God, to comfort all that mourn: To appoint unto them that mourn in Zion, to give unto them beauty for ashes, the oil of joy for mourning, the garment of praise for the spirit of heaviness."

Jesus was a Preacher.

Luke 4:16–21:

"And he came to Nazareth, where he had been brought up: and, as his custom was, he went into the synagogue on the sabbath day, and stood up for to read. And there was delivered unto him the book of the prophet Esaias. And when he had opened the book, he found the place where it was written, The Spirit of the Lord is upon me, because he hath anointed me to preach the gospel to the poor; he hath sent me to heal the brokenhearted, to preach deliverance to the captives, and recovering of sight to the blind, to set at liberty them that are bruised, to preach the acceptable year of the Lord. And he closed the book, and he gave it again to the minister, and sat down. And the eyes of all them that were in the synagogue were fastened on him. And he began to say unto them, This day is this Scripture fulfilled in your ears."

John 3:34:

"For he whom God hath sent speaketh the words of God: for God giveth not the Spirit by measure unto him."

3. TO BE A GREAT LIGHT.

Isa. 49:6:

"I will also give thee for a light to the Gentiles, that thou mayest be my salvation unto the end of the earth."

Isa. 9:2:

"The people that walked in darkness have seen a great light: they that dwell in the land of the shadow of death, upon them hath the light shined."

Isa. 42:6:

"I the Lord have called thee in righteousness, and will hold thine hand; and will keep thee, and give thee for a covenant of the people, for a light of the Gentiles."

JESUS WAS A GREAT LIGHT.

Luke 2:32:

"A light to lighten the Gentiles, and the glory of thy people Israel."

Matt. 4:13-16:

"And leaving Nazareth, he came and dwelt in Capernaum, ... That it might be fulfilled which was spoken by Esaias the prophet, saying, The land of Zabulon, and the land of Nephthalim, by the way of the sea, beyond Jordan, Galilee of the Gentiles: The people which sat in darkness saw great light; and to them which sat in the region and shadow of death light is sprung up."

John 1:7-9:

"The same came for a

witness, to bear witness of the Light, that all men through him might believe. He was not that Light, but was sent to bear witness of that Light. That was the true Light, which lighteth every man that cometh into the world."

John 8:12:

"Then spake Jesus again unto them, saying, I am the light of the world: he that followeth me shall not walk in darkness, but shall have the light of life."

John 9:5:

"As long as I am in the world, I am the light of the world."

4. MESSIAH TO BE A HEALER OF THE AFFLICTED.

Isa. 35:5,6:

"Then the eyes of the blind shall be opened, and the ears of the deaf shall be unstopped. Then shall the lame man leap as a hart, and the tongue of the dumb sing: for in the wilderness shall waters

JESUS WAS A GREAT HEALER.

Matt. 9:28-30:

"And when he was come into the house, the blind men came to him: and Jesus saith unto them, Believe ye that I am able to do this? They said unto him, Yea, Lord. Then touched he their eyes, break out, and streams in the desert."

Isa. 29:18,19:

"And in that day shall the deaf hear the words of the book, and the eyes of the blind shall see out of obscurity, and out of darkness. The meek also shall increase their joy in the Lord, and the poor among men shall rejoice in the Holy One of Israel."

saying, According to your faith be it unto you. And their eyes were opened."

Matt. 11:4,5:

"Jesus answered and said unto them, Go and shew John again those things which ye do hear and see: The blind receive their sight, and the lame walk, the lepers are cleansed, and the deaf hear, the dead are raised up, and the poor have the gospel preached to them."

Matt. 12:22:

"Then was brought unto him one possessed with a devil, blind and dumb: and he healed him."

Matt. 15:30:

"And great multitudes came unto him, having with them lame, blind, dumb, maimed, and many others, and cast them down at Jesus' feet; and he healed them."

John 11:43,44:

"And when he thus had spoken, he cried with a loud voice, Lazarus, come forth. And he that was dead, came forth."

5. To Triumphantly Enter the Jewish Capital.

Zech. 9:9:

"Rejoice greatly, O daughter of Zion; shout, O daughter of Jerusalem: behold, thy King cometh unto thee: he is just, and having salvation; lowly, and riding upon an ass, and upon a colt the foal of an ass."

Triumphal Entry of Jesus.

Matt. 21:1-8:

"And when they drew nigh unto Jerusalem, and were come to Bethphage, unto the mount of Olives, then sent Jesus two disciples, Saying unto them, Go into the village over against you, and straightway ye shall find an ass tied, and a colt with her: loose them, and bring them unto me. And if any man say aught unto you, ye shall say, The Lord hath need of them; and straightway he will send them. All this was done, that it might be fulfilled which was spoken by the prophet, saying, Tell ye the daughter of Sion, Behold, thy King cometh unto thee, meek, and sitting upon an ass, and a colt the foal of an ass. And the disciples went, and did as Jesus commanded them, and brought the ass, and the colt, and put on them their clothes.

Psa. 8:2:
"Out of the mouth of babes and sucklings hast thou ordained strength because of thine enemies, that thou mightest still the enemy and the avenger."

and they set him thereon."

Matt. 21:16:
"And said unto him, Hearest thou what these say? And Jesus saith unto them, Yea; have ye never read, Out of the mouth of babes and sucklings thou hast perfected praise?"

6. HE WILL BE REJECTED.

Isa. 53:3:
"He is despised and rejected of men; a man of sorrows, and acquainted with grief: and we hid as it were our faces from him: he was despised, and we esteemed him not."

JESUS WAS REJECTED.

Matt. 27:22,23:
"Pilate saith unto them, What shall I do then with Jesus which is called Christ? They all say unto him, Let him be crucified. And the governor said, Why, what evil hath he done? But they cried out the more, saying, Let him be crucified."

Mark 15:13,14:
"And they cried out again, Crucify him. Then Pilate said unto them, Why, what evil hath he done? And they cried out the more exceedingly, Crucify him."

Isa. 49:7:
"Thus saith the Lord,

Luke 23:18,20:
"And they cried out all

the Redeemer of Israel, and his Holy One, to him whom man despiseth, to him whom the nation abhorreth."

at once, saying, Away with this man, and release unto us Barabbas: Pilate therefore, willing to release Jesus, spake again unto them. But they cried, saying, Crucify him, crucify him."

John 19:6,15:

"When the chief priests therefore and officers saw him, they cried out, saying, Crucify him, crucify him. Pilate saith unto them, Take ye him, and crucify him: for I find no fault in him: But they cried out, Away with him, away with him, crucify him."

CHAPTER VI.

MESSIAH'S ARREST AND DEATH.

1. THE BETRAYAL.
(1.) THE BETRAYER.
Psa. 41:9:
"Yea, mine own familiar friend, in whom I trusted, which did eat of my bread, hath lifted up his heel against me."

BETRAYAL OF JESUS.
THE BETRAYER.
John 13:26,30:
"Jesus answered, He it is, to whom I shall give a sop, when I have dipped it. And when he had dipped the sop, he gave it to Judas Iscariot, the son of Simon. He then, having received the sop, went immediately out; and it was night."
John 18:2,3:
"And Judas also, which betrayed him, knew the place; . . . . Judas then, having received a band of men . . . . cometh thither with lanterns and torches and weapons."

(2.) THE PRICE PAID.
Zech. 11:12:
"And I said unto them, If ye think good, give me

PRICE PAID FOR JESUS.
Matt. 26:15:
"And said unto them, What will ye give me, and

my price: and if not, forbear. So they weighed for my price *thirty* pieces of silver."

(3.) DISPOSITION OF PRICE PAID.

Zech. 11:13:
"And the Lord said unto me, Cast it unto the potter: a goodly price that I was prized at of them. And I took the thirty pieces of silver, and cast them to the potter in the house of the Lord."

I will deliver him unto you? And they covenanted with him for *thirty* pieces of silver."

DISPOSITION OF PRICE PAID FOR JESUS.

Matt. 27:3-10:
"Then Judas . . . . repented himself, and brought again the *thirty* pieces of silver to the chief priests and elders, saying, I have sinned in that I have betrayed the innocent blood, ... and he cast down the pieces of silver in the temple, and departed, and went and hanged himself. And the chief priests took the silver pieces, and said, It is not lawful for to put them into the treasury, because it is the price of blood. And they took counsel, and bought with them the potter's field; to bury strangers in. . . . . Then was fulfilled that which was spoken by Jeremy the prophet, saying, And they took the *thirty* pieces of silver, the price of him that was valued, whom

they of the children of Israel did value: and gave them for the potter's field, as the Lord appointed me."

(4.) THE SHEPHERD SMITTEN, THE SHEEP SCATTERED.

Zech. 13:7:
"Awake, O sword, against my Shepherd, and against the man that is my fellow, saith the Lord of hosts: smite the Shepherd, and the sheep shall be scattered."

JESUS TAKEN, THE DISCIPLES SCATTERED.

Matt. 26:31:
"Then saith Jesus unto them, All ye shall be offended because of me this night: for it is written, I will smite the Shepherd, and the sheep of the flock shall be scattered abroad."
(Same in Mark 14:27.)

2. THE FALSE WITNESSES.

Psa. 27:12:
"Deliver me not over unto the will of mine enemies: for false witnesses are risen up against me, and such as breathe out cruelty."

Psa. 35:11:
"False witnesses did rise up; they laid to my charge things that I knew not."

FALSE WITNESSES AGAINST JESUS.

Matt. 26:59–61:
"Now the chief priests, and elders, and all the counsel, sought false witness against Jesus, to put him to death: but found none: yea, though many false witnesses came, yet found they none. At the last came two false witnesses, and said, This fellow said, I am able to destroy the temple of God, and to build it in three days."

3. TREATMENT AT THE CROSS.

(1.) WHAT MESSIAH HIMSELF WILL DO.

a. WILL SUFFER FOR OTHERS.

Isa. 53:4,5,12:
"Surely he hath borne our griefs, and carried our sorrows: yet we did esteem him stricken, smitten of God, and afflicted. But he was wounded for our transgressions, he was bruised for our iniquities: the chastisement of our peace was upon him; and with his stripes we are healed. And he bare the sin of many."

TREATMENT OF JESUS AT THE CROSS.

WHAT JESUS DID.

HE SUFFERED FOR OTHERS.

I. Peter 3:18:
"For Christ also hath once suffered for sins, the just for the unjust, that he might bring us to God."

I. Cor. 15:3:
"For I delivered unto you first of all that which I also received, how that Christ died for our sins according to the Scriptures."

Rom. 4:25:
"Who was delivered for our offences.

I. Peter 2:21,24:
"Because Christ also suffered for us. Who his own self bare our sins in his own body on the tree."

II. Cor. 5:21:
"For he hath made him to be sin for us, who knew no sin."

Heb. 9:28:
"So Christ was once of-

fered to bear the sins of many."

Matt. 8:16,17:

"When the evening was come they brought unto him many that were possessed with devils: and he cast out the spirits with his word, and healed all that were sick: That it might be fulfilled which was spoken by Esaias the prophet, saying, Himself took our infirmities, and bare our sicknesses."

b. WILL INTERCEDE FOR HIS PERSECUTORS.

Psa. 109:4:

"For my love they are my adversaries: but I give myself unto prayer."

Isa. 53:12:

"He bare the sin of many, and made intercession for the transgressors."

JESUS PRAYED FOR HIS ENEMIES.

Luke 23:34:

"Father, forgive them; for they know not what they do."

Rom. 8:34:

"Who is he that condemneth? It is Christ that died, yea rather, that is risen again, who is even at the right hand of God, who also maketh intercession for us."

Heb. 7:25:

"Wherefore he is able also to save them to the uttermost that come unto God by him, seeing he ever liveth to make intercession for them."

Heb. 9:24:

"For Christ is not entered into the holy places made with hands, which are the figures of the true: but into heaven itself, now to appear in the presence of God for us."

I. John 2:1:

"And if any man sin, we have an advocate with the Father, Jesus Christ the righteous."

c. WILL CRY UNTO GOD.

Psa. 22:1:

"My God, my God, why hast thou forsaken me? Why art thou so far from helping me?"

JESUS CRIED UNTO GOD.

Matt. 27:46:

"And about the ninth hour Jesus cried with a loud voice, saying, Eli, Eli, lama sabachthani? that is to say, My God, my God, why hast thou forsaken me?"

(Same in Mark 15:34:)

d. WILL DIE WITH MALEFACTORS.

Isa. 53:12:

"And he was numbered with the transgressors."

JESUS DIED WITH MALEFACTORS.

Mark 15:27,28:

"And with him they crucified two thieves.... And the Scripture was fulfilled, which saith, And he was numbered with the transgressors."

Matt. 27:38:
"Then were there two thieves crucified with him; one on the right hand, and another on the left."

Luke 23:33:
"And when they were come to the place, which is called Calvary, there they crucified him, and the malefactors, one on the right hand, and the other on the left."

Luke 22:37:
"For I say unto you, that this that is written must yet be accomplished in me, And he was reckoned among ,the transgressors: For the things concerning me have an end."

(2.) WHAT OTHERS WILL DO TO HIM.

WHAT THEY DID TO JESUS.

a. WILL PIERCE HIS HANDS AND FEET.

JESUS WAS PIERCED.

Psa. 22:16:
"They pierced my hands and my feet."

Zech. 13:6:
"And one shall say unto

John 20:25,27:
"Except I shall see in his hands the print of the nails, and put my finger into the print of the nails,

him, What are these wounds in thine hands?" and thrust my hand into his side, I will not believe. Reach hither thy finger, and behold my hands; and reach hither thy hand, and thrust it into my side; and be not faithless, but believing."

b. WILL GIVE HIM VINEGAR TO DRINK.

Psa. 69:21:

"They gave me also gall for my meat; and in my thirst they gave me vinegar to drink."

THEY GAVE JESUS VINEGAR TO DRINK.

Matt. 27:34:

"They gave him vinegar to drink mingled with gall: and when he had tasted thereof, he would not drink."

Luke 23:36:

"And the soldiers also mocked him, coming to him, and offering him vinegar."

John 19:29:

"Now there was set a vessel full of vinegar: and they filled a sponge with vinegar, and put it upon hyssop, and put it to his mouth."

c. WILL DIVIDE HIS GARMENTS: CAST LOTS FOR HIS COAT.

Psa. 22:18:

"They part my gar-

THEY DIVIDED JESUS' GARMENTS; CAST LOTS FOR HIS COAT.

John 19:23, 24:

"Then the soldiers,

ments among them, and cast lots upon my vesture."

when they .... took his garments, and made four parts, to every soldier a part; and also his coat: now the coat was without seam, ... Let us not rend it, but cast lots for it, whose it shall be: that the Scripture might be fulfilled, which saith, They parted my raiment among them, and for my vesture they did cast lots. These things therefore the soldiers did."

d. THEY BREAK NO BONES, BUT PIERCED HIM.

THEY BROKE NO BONES OF JESUS, BUT PIERCED HIM.

Exod. 12:46:
"Neither shall ye break a bone thereof (i.e., of the passover lamb)."
Num. 9:12:
"They shall leave none of it unto the morning, nor break any bone of it." (The passover lamb.)
Psa. 34:20:
"He keepeth all his bones: not one of them is broken."

Zech. 12:10:
"And they shall look

John 19:32,33,36:
"Then came the soldiers, and brake the legs of the first, and of the other which was crucified with him. But when they came to Jesus, and saw that he was dead already, they brake not his legs. For these things were done, that the Scriptures should be fulfilled, A bone of him shall not be broken."

John 19:37:
"And again another

upon me whom they have pierced."

Scripture saith, They shall look on him whom they pierced."

e. THEY WILL DERIDE MESSIAH.

Psa. 22:6-8:

"But I am a worm, and no man: a reproach of men, and despised of the people. All they that see me laugh me to scorn: they shoot out the lip, they shake the head, saying, he trusted on the Lord that he would deliver him: let him deliver him, seeing he delighted in him."

THEY DERIDED JESUS.

Matt. 27:39-43:

"And they that passed by reviled him, wagging their heads, and saying, Thou that destroyest the temple, and buildest it in three days, save thyself. If thou be the Son of God, come down from the cross. Likewise also the chief priests mocking him, with the scribes and elders, said, he saved others; himself he can not save. If he be the King of Israel, let him now come down from the cross, and we will believe him. He trusted in God; let him deliver him now, if he will have him: for he said, I am the Son of God."

Mark 15:29-32:

"And they that passed by railed on him, wagging their heads, and saying, Ah, thou that destroyest the temple, and buildest it in three days, Save thy-

MESSIAH'S ARREST AND DEATH.

self, and come down from the cross. Likewise also the chief priests mocking said among themselves with the scribes, he saved others; himself he can not save. Let Christ the King of Israel descend now from the cross, that we may see and believe."

f. WILL BURY HIM WITH THE RICH.

Isa. 53:9:

"And he made his grave with the wicked, and with the rich in his death."

JESUS WAS BURIED WITH THE RICH.

Matt. 27:57f.

"At even, ... came a rich man .... and laid it in his own new tomb."

(Same is in Mark 15: 43–46.)

CHAPTER VII.

MESSIAH TO RISE FROM THE DEAD.

1. WOULD NEVER SEE CORRUPTION.

Psa. 16:10:

"For thou wilt not leave my soul in hell; (See Part I.) neither wilt thou suffer thine Holy One to see corruption."

JESUS NEVER SAW CORRUPTION.

Acts 2:27,31:

"Because thou wilt not leave my soul in hell (See Part I.), neither wilt thou suffer thine Holy One to see corruption. He, seeing this before, spake of the resurrection of Christ, that his soul was not left in hell, neither his flesh did see corruption.'"

Acts 13:34,35:

"And as concerning that he raised him up from the dead, now no more to return to corruption, he said on this wise, I will give you the sure mercies of David. Wherefore he saith also in another psalm, Thou shalt not suffer thine Holy One to see corruption."

Luke 24:6,46:

"He is not here, but is risen: remember how he

spake unto you when he was yet in Galilee. And said unto them, Thus it is written, and thus it behooved Christ to suffer, and to rise from the dead the third day."
Mark 16:6:
"And he saith unto them. Be not affrighted: ye seek Jesus of Nazareth, which was crucified: he is risen; he is not here."
Matt. 28:6
"He is not here: for he is risen, as he said."

2. HIS ASCENSION.

Psa. 68:18:
"Thou hast ascended on high, thou hast led captivity captive; thou hast received gifts for men."

ASCENSION OF JESUS.

Acts 1:9:
"And when he had spoken these things, while they beheld, he was taken up: and a cloud received him out of their sight."
Luke 24:51:
"And it came to pass, while he blessed them, he was parted from them, and carried up into heaven."

Psa. 24:7:
"Lift up your heads, O ye gates; and be ye lifted up, ye everlasting doors; and the King of glory shall come in."

Mark 16:19:
"So then, after the Lord had spoken unto them, he was received up into heaven, and sat on the right hand of God."

CHAPTER VIII.

HIS KINGDOM TO GROW.

1. HIS KINGDOM TO BE A MISSIONARY KINGDOM.

Psa. 72:8:

"He shall have dominion also from sea to sea, and from the river unto the ends of the earth."

Psa. 2:8:

"Ask of me, and I shall give thee the heathen for thine inheritance, and the uttermost parts of the earth for thy possession."

Zech. 9:10:

"And his dominion shall be from sea even to sea, and from the river even to the ends of the earth."

JESUS' KINGDOM IS MISSIONARY.

Luke 24:47:

"And that repentance and remission of sins should be preached in his name among all nations, beginning at Jerusalem."

Mark 16:15:

"And he said unto them, Go ye into all the world, and preach the gospel to every creature."

2. TO BE PROPAGATED BY HIS CONVERTS.

Isa. 52:10:

"The Lord hath made bare his holy arm in the eyes of all the nations; and all the ends of the earth shall see the salvation of our God."

JESUS' KINGDOM SO PROPAGATED.

Matt. 28:19:

"Go ye (disciples) therefore, and teach all nations, baptizing them in the name of the Father, and of the Son, and of the Holy Ghost."

www.ingramcontent.com/pod-product-compliance
Lightning Source LLC
Chambersburg PA
CBHW032154160426
43197CB00008B/915